P9-AFC-865

Using the Body to Enlighten the Mind

Dahnhak Kigong

Using the Body to Enlighten the Mind

Dahnhak Kigong

Healing Society
6560 Highway 179, Ste.114
Sedona, AZ 86351
www.healingsociety.com
1–877–504–1106

Library Congress Control Number: 2004109076
ISBN-10: 1–932843–01–9
ISBN-13: 978–1–932843–01–9

Translated by Daniel Graham
Designed by Pishion
Printed in South Korea

If you are unable to order this book
from your local bookstores, you may
order through www.healingsociety.com
or www.amazon.com.

Using the Body to Enlighten the Mind

Dahnhak Kigong

ILCHI LEE

Healing Society

Ilchi Lee, founder of Dahnhak Ki-gong

Author's Preface

Many people believe that the twenty first century will be the era of Ki, the life force of the universe. As evidence for this assertion, we find ourselves awash in a sea of healing methods, training practices, and products related to the application of Ki. The word Ki has become familiar to many people. When it comes to sensing and using Ki directly, however, many people still believe it is difficult and mysterious and something that only special people can experience.

We all possess the ability to sense Ki. Awakening sensitivity to Ki is natural, like gaining a sense of balance when learning to ride a bicycle, or acquiring the ability to float when learning how to swim. For more than twenty years, I have been helping many people develop awareness of the true life within us all. Dahnhak Ki-gong is a training method designed to help people experience the true life within them directly with their bodies, not with their heads. This occurs through the medium of Ki.

I have previously published *Meridian Exercises for Self-healing*. This fall into the category of Ki-gong, and contain important health practices handed down in Asia from ancient times. I organized them into a system that modern people can easily use. Infused with the spirit and principles of Dahnhak, they are a modern adaptation of the Taoist Shin-seon-do ideology that was the basis of the philosophy of the Korean people.

Dahnhak Ki-gong, based on the principles and philosophy of Creation (Jo-hwa), Education (Gyo-hwa), and Civilization (Chi-hwa), served as the foundation for an enlightened community in Korean antiquity. The concept that there are three intrinsic elements of harmony, Chun-ji-in Sam-jae, is a universal principle of life in which humanity, nature, and the cosmos blend together, as opposed to the view of a dichotomous structure of competition and confrontation. This manifested as a profound philosophy of life through which enlightenment found a place in the social system. Dahnhak Ki-gong is one of the methodologies for training many people in the ability to concretely experience and manifest peace.

It gives me great joy to see our once forgotten philosophy and training methods recognized for their true value among people all over the world, including the United States, Japan, Canada, the United Kingdom, Brazil, and Korea. This is a result not only of the physical and mental effects of Dahnhak Ki-gong, but also of the shining light of the philosophy and spirit it contains. As we publish this book, I earnestly hope that many more people will find harmony of body and mind through Dahnhak Ki-gong, and that genuine peace on earth will manifest through a recovery of harmony between humanity and nature.

Ilchi Lee
July 2004, Sedona, Arizona

Contents

Chapter 1

Understanding Dahnhak Ki-gong

丹學氣功

Those whose hearts are bright like the sun know
they have heaven and earth within them.

-From Chun-bu-kyung

1. What Is Dahnhak Ki-gong?

Mind-Body Training Methods Containing Philosophy of Ancient Korea

The empty sky at which we look with no particular thoughts in mind is not just empty space. It looks empty, but it is full of the life energy, Ki. Every one of us lives and breathes depending on that empty sky. Although Ki is invisible, it is the dynamic force creating all organisms including humans, making them active and changing them.

The Korean people called the source of life, "Han," and also named the primordial life force or energy, "Dahn." Dahnhak Ki-gong is a mind-body training method based on the "Han Philosophy" of ancient Korea.

The Han Philosophy contains the truth that everything in the universe was created from "One Ki" and also returns to this one place when extinguished, and that everything is connected by that one energy source. It also includes the idea that the universe comprises three intrinsic elements, heaven, earth, and humanity, and that these three do not exist separately from each other.

Our bodies and minds are not separate, either. The mind can be trained by governing the body, and the body can be trained by controlling the mind. The role of Ki is to connect body and mind like a bridge at a point between the two. Dahnhak Ki-gong is a practice for maximizing the capabilities of the body and mind by accepting and controlling the life force of the infinite universe, Ki, through concentration, Ki-gong movements, and breathing.

Ki Exercises for Recovering Naturalness of Life

Each movement in Dahnhak Ki-gong was created by standardizing movements that come out naturally with the flow of energy when one is in a deep state of meditation. When body and mind become one in this energy, this oneness may express itself in dance. It may manifest in the form of martial arts movements, and appear in a variety of forms, such as vibrations and the hand gestures of Buddhist images.

Although it involves turning over our bodies to the flow of energy, Dahnhak Ki-gong also consists of controlling the energy flow as we desire. These attitudes seem contrary to each other, but with depth of practice comes the knowledge that the two are linked as one.

Learning to use Ki is like learning to swim. The buoyancy of water, like Ki energy, is invisible and cannot be touched, but the instant we learn to use it, we can swim freely and move as we want. Even without studying Ki-gong, once we learn to use the current of the essential life within us, it flows from our bodies on its own. This is a natural phenomenon of life, like a fish playing in the water where it lives.

When we live in accordance with the natural flow of life, our bod-

Won-bang-gak (circle-square-triangle) Image

Symbolizing Chun-ji-in (heaven-earth-human) thought, this figure signifies harmony. Its shape expresses the coexistence of heaven, earth, and humanity, with the circle representing the round vault of heaven, the square indicating the jagged earth, and the triangle signifying humankind. This symbol was often used in traditional Korean patterns and designs, and can be seen in places such as the frames of paper sliding doors and architectural forms.

ies maintain optimal health, and our minds become bright, positive, and peaceful. The Korean people used the word "Yullyeo" to indicate a state of harmony within the natural rhythm and order of life. Dahnhak Ki-gong is training for bringing this Yullyeo to life. When this vital awareness in our bodies comes to life, our bodies themselves discriminate between what is bad and what is good for us. Even if our bodies are temporarily in a state of disharmony, they purify themselves of factors of imbalance to achieve a harmonious state.

Various illnesses are cured and we do not readily become sick in the process of practicing Dahnhak Ki-gong because our bodies' immune systems are strengthened, maximizing their natural healing abilities.

Origin of Dahnhak Ki-gong

Most modern systems of Ki-gong came from China, and many people believe Ki-gong originated there. Its beginnings, however, can also be found in the Shin-seon-do (Taoist practices) of Korea.

Based on the ancient text *Han-dahn Ko-gi*, we can see that Ki-gong began with the history of the Korean people. The *Han-dahn Ko-gi* relates that Emperor Han-in, who lived in Central Asia about 10,000 years ago, awakened to the divine nature of humanity through the practice of Shin-seon-do.

Shin-seon-do is not a simple health method or martial art, but a discipline for awakening to the deep principles of the universe by training the body and mind, a practice for becoming one with the cosmos to grow as a complete human being who lives for the good of all people and all life.

The lineage associated with these practices reached later generations, along with the principles of the *Chun-bu-kyung*, and created a community centered on Mt. Baekdu that revealed the divinity of

Yullyeo

There is an autonomous regulating action within the currents of the cosmos, a healing ability, a power that seeks to return to the source. This driving force moving the universe, this essential power, we call "Yullyeo." Yullyeo is expressed as light, sound, and vibration.

Ji-gam, Jo-sik, Geum-chok

According to the *Han-dahn Ko-gi*, records indicate that ancient ascetics developed their bodies and minds through the practice of three methods: Ji-gam, Jo-sik, and Geum-chok. Ji-gam trains the mind to calm the thoughts and emotions and Jo-sik trains the breath to regulate energy through breathing. Geum-chok is a practice for entering a deep spiritual world beyond the five senses.

humanity. By the time of Dangun Chosun, these practices had been concretely developed into a founding ideology of the humanitarian ideal, "Hong-ik In-gan I-hwa Se-gye." Dangun Chosun, based on the principles of creation, education, and civilization, widely spread the philosophy and practices of Shin-seon-do, resulting in the dominant influence of Taoism in that time.

The practice of Ji-gam, Jo-sik, and Geum-chok, related in the *Sam-il-shin-go*, one of the three great scriptures of the Korean people, in particular form the basis of Shin-seon-do practice. This Shin-seon-do practice spread to the various peoples of Asia, including China, and developed into a variety of Ki-gong methods. Its lineage was broken with the collapse of Dangun Chosun, however, and the spirit and philosophy it contained were also diluted and faded gradually with time; until today only its technical aspects were handed down in various forms.

Differences between Dahnhak Ki-gong and Chinese Qigong

Chinese Qigong developed through focusing on techniques: into health Qigong for health, longevity, and immortality, and martial Qigong for self-defense and controlling an opponent. Stressing the technical aspects of these arts has led Chinese Qigong to achieve brilliant growth in the field of medical Qigong, but the philosophy contained in these systems has faded by comparison. The difference between Chinese Qigong and Dahnhak Ki-gong, in short, is the difference between Taoist techniques and the Way.

Dahnhak Ki-gong has developed into a modern, scientific system the philosophy and difficult training methods of Shin-seon-do, the lineage of which had been broken in the past. The fundamental goal of Dahnhak Ki-gong goes beyond training body and mind to awak-

Chun-bu-kyung

The *Chun-bu-kyung* is the oldest of Korean scriptures, transmitted by word-of-mouth since the time of Emperor Hanin. Along with *Cham-jun-gye-gyung* and *Sam-il-shin-go*, it is one of the three great scriptures of the Korean people. Comprising 81 Chinese characters, *Chun-bu-kyung* uses numbers to express the birth and death of the universe and the principle of evolutionary creation.

It contains the cosmic principle that creation and evolution take place in a time with no beginning and no end, from the birth of humanity to its death, and that, in the end, by achieving the perfection of humanity, we complete our mission as living beings born on this earth.

en us to the true purpose and truths of our lives as human beings and to manifest this purpose in the world.

When we awaken to the living energy within ourselves and achieve harmony of body and mind, our efforts to put these principles into practice and live in harmony with the world are supported. Only then is the true consummation of Dahnhak Ki-gong finally achieved.

These are some of the 24 techniques of sitting medi-taion, which influenced the development of Taoist health cultivation methods into medical meridian exer-cises ▶

These pictures show one current of Chinese martial Qigong ▶

2. Types of Dahnhak Ki-gong

Jung-gong and Dong-gong:
Training in Stillness and Motion

There are generally two types of Ki-gong. The practice of controlling breathing and concentrating the mind while performing movements is called Dong-gong, and the method of adopting a specific posture while controlling breathing and concentrating the mind without moving is called Jung-gong. All forms of Dahnhak Ki-gong introduced here are of the Dong-gong type, but they can also be used to practice Jung-gong by stopping and holding a posture for a period of time.

Practice is divided into Dong-gong and Jung-gong according to whether we move the body during training, but strictly speaking, this is only an external classification. Even in a state of Jung-gong, energy constantly enters and leaves our bodies as we repeatedly inhale and exhale. We quietly entrust our bodies to the flow of energy even as we move them vigorously in Dahn-gong. In either case, the result is a state of calm stillness. What is important when we practice Ki-gong is that, even in motion, we must be able to feel stillness, and that, even in stillness, we watch our ceaseless breathing and changing energy to achieve harmony with it.

Jung-gong (Left)

Jung-gong, which generally focuses on Dahn-jon breathing and mental concentration, can cause serious side effects if practitioners concentrate excessively. Expert guidance is absolutely essential for beginners.

Dong-gong (Right)

Dong-gong, while virtually free of side effects, provides mental stability through concentration and physical health through proper exercise, making it particularly appropriate for modern people, who do not get enough exercise

Types of Dahnhak Ki-gong

The movements of Dahnhak Ki-gong are a standardization of those following the flow of Ki that bursts forth from a deep state of meditation. Other programs have systematized this flow into a certain form to help many people train their bodies and minds in a way that is easier and more fun. These programs are Dahn-mu, Dahn-gong, Chun-bu Shin-gong, Ilchi Ki-gong, Earth Dahn-gong, and Un-ki Shim-gong. Here we introduce Dahn-gong Gi-bon-hyung (Basic Form) and Chuk-ki-hyung (Ki Accumulation Form), which build the basics of Dahnhak Ki-gong, and Ilchi Ki-gong, which allows modern people to delve into the exquisiteness of Ki-gong easily and in depth.

When Ji-gam (energy sensitivity) practice deepens and a person comes to feel the flow of energy, the dance-like movements of Dahn-mu manifest themselves. If Ki flows strongly during Dahn-mu, this develops into the forceful, rhythmic movements of Dahn-gong, which are like those seen in the martial arts. Any practitioner can re-create limitless Ki-gong methods once he or she becomes adept at feeling the natural flow of energy during the movements. This natural creativity is one of the most significant characteristics of Dahnhak Ki-gong.

Ilchi Ki-gong in particular can be practiced by beginner and Ki-gong veteran alike, each according to his or her perseverance and endurance. Movements may be performed both quickly and slowly, depending on the breathing of the person doing the training. Movements performed softly become a dance; performed strongly, they can transform into martial-art or self-defense techniques.

Our bodies experience disease due to blocked meridians and poor Ki and blood circulation caused by a state of imbalance generally resulting from spinal or skeletal misalignment. Dahn-gong Gi-bon-hyung is a training method that corrects skeletal misalignment and builds the basic stamina that allows the practitioner to train Ki-gong in earnest once the basics of the postures are in place and the body is strengthened. Dahn-gong Chuk-ki-hyung trains the lower body, making it strong and firm, and fills the Dahn-jon with energy to perfect the so-called "Sang-heo Ha-sil" posture, in which the lower body is solid while the upper body is relaxed.

Once we accumulate Ki to a certain extent through Dahn-gong Chuk-ki-hyung, we train internal Ki through Chun-bu Shin-gong or Ilchi Ki-gong. Chun-bu Shin-gong and Ilchi Ki-gong cause energy accumulated in the Dahn-jon to circulate through the entire body, to build up in the bones and sinews, and to penetrate deeply into the bones. With deepening practice, we reach a stage where energy circulates freely in the body as its six major joints open up. Furthermore, we experience a state of oneness with the universe as the energy in our bodies and the universe flows and circulates through us unrestrictedly.

3. Principles of Dahnhak Ki-gong Training

Su-Seung Hwa-Gang: Water Ascends, Fire Descends

Everything in the universe achieves harmony through the circulation of two kinds of energy, Yin and Yang. Our bodies are the same. In our bodies, the energy of water, which corresponds to Yin, originates in the kidneys, and the energy of fire, which corresponds to Yang, starts in the heart. Water energy from the kidneys rises along the Governor Vessel (Dok-maek) to clear the head, and fire energy from the heart sinks along the Conception Vessel (Im-maek) to the Dahn-jon and warms the lower abdomen. When this happens, our bodies achieve harmony and maintain a state of optimum health.

When we are overly anxious, enraged, or plagued by troublesome thoughts, our mouths become very dry and our saliva takes on a bitter taste as the Conception Vessel is blocked. With the Conception Vessel blocked, fire energy from the heart, unable to circulate downward, rises upward and breaks the Yin-Yang balance within the body as it burns off water energy.

Water energy ascends and fire energy descends naturally in our bodies when our minds are settled and at peace. When this happens, our mouths fill with a sweet saliva, called "Ok-su." We are filled with even more energy and our minds become even clearer if we swallow this saliva.

Dahnhak Ki-gong facilitates this process in the human body. What the practitioner should keep foremost in mind, therefore, is not to let sudden rage or excessive anxiety or worry squander harmonious energy carefully cultivated through training.

Ascending Water energy, Descending Fire energy and Conception, Governor Vessel Flow

The Dahn-jon must be strengthened to ensure that water energy ascends and fire energy descends as they should. If we are subjected to excessive stress or think too hard when the Dahn-jon is weak, fire energy rises, disturbing the natural flow of energy.

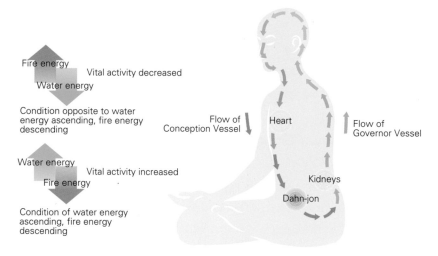

Fire energy
Vital activity decreased
Water energy

Condition opposite to water energy ascending, fire energy descending

Water energy
Vital activity increased
Fire energy

Condition of water energy ascending, fire energy descending

Flow of Conception Vessel
Heart
Flow of Governor Vessel
Kidneys
Dahn-jon

Jung-Choong Ki-Jang Shin-Myung:
Jung Is Full, Ki Is Mature, and Shin Is Awakened

The words Jung, Ki, and Shin refer to grades of vital energy in our bodies. As energy moves from Jung to Ki, and from Ki to Shin, it becomes purer. Since ancient times, these three kinds of energy have been called the three treasures of the human body, and practitioners consider them very important.

All human energy starts as Jung in the Lower Dahn-jon. Jung signifies the primal life force and corresponds to sexual energy. Since
ancient times, practitioners have considered the Jung energy in their
bodies to be very precious and warned against wasting it carelessly.
Once it has reached a state of fullness, Jung is sublimated and con-
verted into Ki.

The Middle Dahn-jon is activated once it is filled with energy
and Ki develops. This means that Ki matures. When Ki fills the
Dahn-jon, energy circulates smoothly through our bodies and the
Conception Vessel in the chest is opened. If we lack energy or it fails
to circulate smoothly, the energy of the Middle Dahn-jon contracts.
The Middle Dahn-jon is the seat of the soul and the place where our
true nature resides. When the Middle Dahn-jon comes alive, ethical
speech and behavior well up from within, regardless of our inten-
tions. With the development of mature Ki, this energy is sublimated
and becomes Shin.

When Jung is full and Ki matures, Shin is awakened. When Shin is
awakened, wisdom and creative insight grow and reason is sharp-
ened as the Upper Dahn-jon develops. However, Shin cannot display
its power alone, and must unite with Jung and Ki to operate. Once

Shin

Ki

Jung

Concepts			Action	Essence	Factors Wasting Energy ⇒ Phenomena	Attitude ⇒ Effects
Korean	Dahnhak	Western				
Yeong	Shin	Spirit	Thinking	Purity, Clarity	Excessive Thinking, Busy Thoughts ⇒ Increased Drowsiness	Attitude of Reverence for Heaven ⇒ Development of Wisdom and Insight
Hon	Ki	Mind	Judgment	Truth, Light	Feebleness of Character, Excessive Talkativeness ⇒ Gluttony (Needs Unsatisfied)	Attitude of Trust, Generosity, Freedom from Avarice ⇒ Warm Humanity, Virtue
Baek	Jung	Body	Drive	Integrity, Cleanness of Character	Overwork, Excessive Exercise and Sexual Activity ⇒ Decreased Libido, Decreased Desire to Work	Integrity, Drive ⇒ Confidence and Courage

Shin is awakened by the pure love welling up from within us, we reach a stage where we can correctly determine how we should live as human beings and how we are able to control our minds to achieve this purpose.

Shim-Ki-Hyul-Jung: Mind Energy Blood Body

**Mind Creates Ki
Ki Creates Mind**

Although energy does proceed from the mind, the mind also arises out of energy. In other words, energy is gathered through concentration of the mind, but the mind is also created by energy. This is what is meant by "Mind creates Ki; Ki creates mind." Although the power of intention can change energy, our minds are also affected by the surrounding environment. We feel joy when we listen to thrilling music; our minds become peaceful and our emotions are enriched when we find ourselves in clean, beautiful environments. Accordingly, it is important to keep our surroundings neat and clean to create an appropriate environment for training.

Shim-Ki-Hyul-Jung means that, "Where mind (consciousness) lies, energy flows, bringing blood and transforming the body." It implies that consciousness is the true reality behind the reality of form.

Arousing internal Ki during Ki-gong practice to create Jin-ki (energy that generated through deep, concentrated breathing) is done through the "power of the mind" based on this principle of Shim-Ki-Hyul-Jung. Accumulating Jin-ki in the body is yet another important role played by the mind. "Ui-su Dahn-jon," or focusing awareness on the Dahn-jon to gather Ki, is based on the same principle. This is why, among the three elements of Ki-gong practice, the method of concentration called "Jo-shim-bup," or mind control, is treated as particularly important.

The mind is like empty space. In the absence of movement, it is completely empty, quiet and unbounded. When we move our minds, however, the Ki, blood, and spirit of our bodies moves with it, and infinite creation unfolds within.

Although strong intent and continuous, repeated thoughts can take material form. In other words, energy gathers where we place our minds, and when energy gathers, blood flows well and vital activity is invigorated, creating our bodies' jeong. This principle applies not only to the bodies of people, but also to the human societies and universe in which we live.

4. Three Elements of Dahnhak Ki-gong Training

Harmony of Movement, Breathing, and Awareness

Harmony of movement, breathing, and awareness is needed for the effective practice of Ki-gong. These are called "Jo-shin (body control)," "Jo-sik (breath control)," and "Jo-shim (mind control)." These three elements are the basics of Dahn-gong practice. We can train Ki-gong correctly only if these three are harmonized appropriately.

Although one of either movement, breathing or awareness, is emphasized occasionally, this does not mean that the other two elements can be ignored. It is difficult to delve deeply into this practice if we are negligent about even one of these elements. Generally, we learn movements first, feel Ki in the movements once we become proficient at them, and then control Ki through breathing and awareness, in that order.

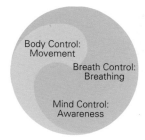

Body Control: Movement

Breath Control: Breathing

Mind Control: Awareness

Trinity of Body, Breath, and Mind Control

Body Control |
Practice correct posture and movements.

Body control means correcting movements and posture to achieve balance and harmony in the body. Correct posture and movements are directly connected with the effects of practice, and act as important elements in ensuring an appropriate balance between the accumulation and circulation of Ki.

Dahnhak Ki-gong is characterized by training that uses the centerline of the human body as an axis to achieve good balance in the muscles and skeleton, top and bottom, left and right. When training, we ensure that the weight of our bodies is always placed right over our center of gravity, and that we do not tilt our bodies to one side, or raise or lower them. Most basic to achieving body control are appropriate tension and relaxation. The trick is to move slowly and softly, tensing, as little as possible, only those muscles necessary for movement while relaxing all other muscles. Adopting correct posture for body control is important, but careshould be should be taken to avoid being overly focused on the movements, which actually causes muscle tension.

Basic Posture for Body Control		
	Head and Neck	Lightly tuck your chin inward so that a vertical line is formed connecting the ears and the Baek-hoe at the crown of the head.
	Eyes	Look toward the front keeping your line of sight level, as if staring off into the distance.
	Mouth and Tongue	Close your mouth so that your lips touch lightly. Be careful not to clinch your teeth. Smile gently, and lightly touch the tip of your tongue to the gum behind your upper teeth.
	Shoulders and Arms	Relax your shoulders and let your arms hang down, leaving some space in your armpits.
	Hands	Open your hands, spreading the fingers naturally.
	Chest and Back	Relax the muscles of your chest naturally so that your back is not arched, and ensure that there is plenty of space between your left and right shoulder blades.
	Abdomen and Waist (Spine)	Do not push out your abdomen, and straighten your waist and spine.

Breath Control | Breathe evenly.

Breath control refers to breathing evenly and naturally, according to one's own lung capacity. When we first practice Ki-gong, we breathe the most comfortably and naturally. In the case of beginners, focusing too much attention on breathing actually prevents relaxation of the muscles and internal organs. Rather than trying too hard to breathe deeply, the practitioner should breathe naturally, quietly, and calmly, without really thinking about it. Deep, even breathing takes place later, once a person reaches a higher level.

The breathing method commonly used in Dahnhak Ki-gong is the natural breathing we use in everyday life. With growing proficiency, all we have to do is choose the breathing method appropriate for ourselves, such as abdominal or Dahn-jon breathing. Going too far in trying to do abdominal or Dahn-jon breathing before we are ready is actually dangerous. It is possible to develop the inversion of Ki which involves congestion and rushing of blood to the head, particularly when the Conception Vessel has considerable blockage. Doing a great deal of breathing from the chest is effective in such cases. We get relief if we breathe deeply when we feel a heaviness in the chest. This is chest breathing. Although chest breathing is effective for invigorating lung function, we cannot expect this alone to cause energy to sink to the Dahn-jon or to increase the energy that extends out to the tips of our fingers and toes.

Location of Breathing and Breathing Methods ▼

Chest Breathing

Abdominal Breathing

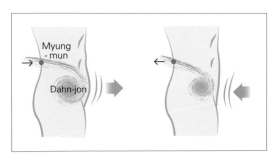

Dahn-jon Breathing

Abdominal breathing is a method by which, when we inhale, the area above and below the navel bulges out simultaneously, and there is tension above the navel and in the spine, as well. With Dahn-jon breathing, when we inhale, only the area below the navel protrudes with some tension, but the spine straightens out without tension. During Dahn-jon Breathing, when we breathe in, we can feel spiraling energy entering the Dahn-jon through the Myeong-mun, and when we breathe out, we can feel energy leaving by the same route.

Mind Control | Control awareness.

Mind control means governing Ki by focusing and controlling awareness. Learning how to control Ki, ultimately, is learning how to control the mind. To achieve mind control, we must first free our minds of busy thoughts. For people first beginning this practice, sitting quietly, emptying the mind of busy thoughts and concentrating the awareness is not easy. This is the Jung-gong approach. Dong-gong, in which the practitioner assumes specific postures and concentrates his or her awareness on movement and breathing, is much more effective for freeing the mind of busy thoughts and achieving unity of body and consciousness to reach a state free from all ideas and thoughts. Another way to achieve mind control is to gather Ki by focusing the awareness on a specific part of the body, such as the hands, the Dahn-jon, or the chest. Yet another method is using intention to cause Ki to flow along the meridians. Mind control, however, is not applicable only when we do Ki-gong. Even if the mind is quieted and comes under control during training, energy is bound to be wasted and scattered when the mind is confused and the awareness is fragmented in everyday life.

The ultimate objective Dahnhak Ki-gong seeks to achieve through mind control is cultivating the ability to train and control our minds so that we can maintain a clear, calm mindset even as we come face-to-face with the difficulties of our everyday lives.

5. Characteristics of Dahnhak Ki-gong

Principle of Rotation |
Many movements are smooth and circular.

The movements of Dahnhak Ki-gong are smooth and circular compared with other systems of Ki-gong. Most hand and leg motions are so circular they seem dancelike. This is because many of the movements are based on the principle of rotation. Sports ordinarily involve many linear body movements. The muscles and joints may actually suffer injury if these are taken to an extreme. Dahnhak Ki-gong, however, employs both linear and curved rotational movements. Its power is a harmony of soft strength and strong softness.

Rotational movement is a phenomenon of life. The earth rotates as it revolves around a rotating sun, and even the innumerable stars in the sky rotate each in their own way. The human body, as a microcosm, follows the principles and laws of the cosmos to the letter.

Each of the joints in the body are designed to rotate, and the DNA contained in each of the body's cells has a rotating helical structure.

The principle of rotation is applied in the practice of Ki-gong, as well. We must perform rotational movements to move Ki deep into our bones. Rotating the bones moves Ki deep into the capillaries. By rotating the joints of our wrists, shoulders, hips, knees, ankles, neck, and waist, we cause friction between bones and generate hot energy. Jin-ki then circulates deep within the bones, and muscles and bones are filled with energy and rejuvenated.

Rotational movement of galaxy (left) and double helix structure of DNA (right)

Circulation of Ki through Angles (Twisting) |
Even beginners feel energy readily.

The use of angles in Ki-gong is similar in many ways to their application in body control. In Ki-gong movements, even minuscule changes in angles allow blocked Ki to circulate and also affect muscle relaxation and respiration rates.

Most movements in Dahnhak Ki-gong are easy and simple, but their effects are very great. Practicing breathing while performing movements that involve angling and then relaxing the fingers, wrists, knees, etc., allows even beginners to feel Ki easily, and is also effective for training internal Ki.

As we advance in years, our bodies age as their muscles and cells lump together and harden. Poor Ki and blood circulation is the reason for this. Although psychological stress is also a factor, Ki and blood circulation is hindered by the long-term effects of poor posture and inadequate or excessive exercise. The muscles connected to the shoulders, hips, arms and legs in particular are frequently subjected to excessive tension or are overextended. In this state, energy fails to circulate deep into the muscles even with exercise.

If we practice breathing and movements that involve rotating the bones and twisting the muscles, waste materials stagnating in the body are effectively eliminated and new energy is delivered deep into the muscles. Movements that twist and squeeze the muscles also activate the capillaries, invigorating Ki and blood circulation.

Movements Using Angles to Circulate Ki

Angling the wrists, ankles, knees, elbows and other joints facilitates Ki circulation. Merely raising the little finger slightly to give it an angle causes Ki to circulate to the entire body.

6. Effects of Dahnhak Ki-gong

Dahnhak Ki-gong causes energy to circulate to every corner of the body through the meridians, blood vessels, and nerves. Once energy circulates throughout the entire body, the chest begins to feel comfortable as the functions of the internal organs are improved and the mind is cleared and refreshed. Swallowing the sweet saliva that is produced at this time results in the natural healing of most diseases in the body. Mentally, as we become linked to the energy source of the infinite universe, various potentials manifest themselves in us.

Internal muscles are trained by movements that are natural and slow, like flowing water, and by movements that are occasionally powerful, like thunder and lightning. A feeling of heat is generated in our bodies in the process of doing these movements, and cold, harmful Ki that has penetrated deep within our bones is driven from our bodies by Jin-ki. If we constantly repeat this process, once blocked energy channels are opened up, blood circulation becomes smooth and regular, the blood itself is cleared of impurities, and, consequently, our minds also become clear.

Once the human body is filled with internal Ki and Jin-ki, its vital activities and natural healing ability are maximized, muscles and cells that have hardened and lost flexibility recover their vitality, the body is purified, and its constitution is changed.

Our natural temperament is closely connected with our internal organs. When our organs are healthy and our energy becomes harmonious, our temperaments also become amicable and harmonious. Furthermore, our eyes are opened to a deep love for the world and humanity. Dahnhak Ki-gong allows us to recover the true body and mind of humanity. The following is a brief summary of the physical and mental effects of Dahnhak Ki-gong.

Physical Effects

- Aligns and strengthens muscles and skeleton.
- Improves blood circulation and warms hands and feet.
- Eliminates fatigue and improves sleep.
- Provides complete recovery from minor illnesses and significant improvement or complete healing of chronic illnesses.
- Creates ability to prevent disease.
- Controls weight and blood pressure.
- Gives the voice strength and confidence.
- Makes the body surprisingly supple.
- Softens skin and eliminates discoloration, freckles, and age spots.
- Menstruation becomes regular and constipation, diarrhea, etc. are normalized.
- Provides overflowing vigor and vitality and contributes to a healthy sex life.
- Brings excessive drinking under control and eliminates hangovers.
- Improves allergy-prone constitutions.
- Martial artists cultivate profound martial skills.

Mental Effects

- Gradually eliminates anxiety, fear, and obsessive thoughts.
- Our minds are put at ease and we feel happiness and peace.
- Changes negative people who lack confidence, making them positive and outgoing.
- Changes uptight people, making them calm and carefree.
- Teaches us to love and care for our bodies.
- Develops courage and boldness.
- Develops concentration and creativity.
- Teaches us to experience and appreciate the infinite power of love filling us.
- Makes us natural, polite people in our personal relationships.
- Changes extreme, aggressive people, making them tender and agreeable.
- Lets us experience a connection of oneness with the universe.

Straightening the Body

Straightening the body actually means keeping the right mind and right attitude. Have no shame in your mind. Straighten your body, and stand tall in the world. When you do not have the right mind, you tend to hide and carry things out secretly. This will lead you to wander in agony and suffering, resulting in the weakening of physical power and energy. Therefore, those who are enlightened straighten their bodies and are always composed, while those who do not have right mind bend their bodies over and try to please others.

- From *Cham-jun-gye-gyung*

Chapter 2

Preparation

丹學氣功

This breath I breathe is no longer my own.
It is the breath of the universe, the breath of life...
When breath enters my body, I am born a new creature;
when breath leaves my body, my old,
sickly self dies.

-By Dr. Ilchi Lee

1. Feeling Ki Makes Ki-gong More Enjoyable

Ji-gam

When we practice Ki-gong, it is essential that we learn Ki awareness. If we practice Dahnhak Ki-gong without feeling any energy, it becomes nothing more than a simple dance or physical exercise.

Although some people think it is very difficult to feel this energy, everyone has a sense for feeling Ki. We are able to smell the fragrance of a flower because we have this Ki sense. Catching a cold is our body's response to broken Ki balance. Learning Ki is like learning to feel the buoyancy of water when we swim or to have a sense of balance when we ride a bicycle.

If we are to feel Ki, we should not approach it through rational logic or analysis. The secret to feeling Ki is concentration. Most people, however, try to understand things analytically, even when they "concentrate." First of all, to feel Ki, we must put aside for a moment our rational thinking and focus on the sensations of our bodies.

When we put a hand in hot water, we instantly feel the heat and pull it out. Although no longer than the blink of an eye, that instant is a state of complete concentration from which our emotions and thoughts are excluded.

Dahnhak Ki-gong has Ji-gam training, which is a very simple method even beginners can use to feel Ki and concentrate. This Ji-gam program can develop their concentration and make training more fun.

Ji-gam signifies "stopping sensation." Here, "stopping sensation" means to stop feeling emotions and thinking thoughts. Normally, our minds are always full of commotion; they are busy vortices of innumerable thoughts, memories, and emotions. If we intentionally try to drive away such busy thoughts and concentrate, even more thoughts come pouring into our minds, one after another. An effective way to concentrate is to find the center of our minds, leaving all such thoughts alone rather than trying hard to eliminate them. If we concentrate exclusively on the feeling of energy, we find that our minds have focused on one place, and that all those busy thoughts have settled down on their own.

The first stage of Ji-gam is recognizing the fact that Ki energy exists. It is important that we believe in Ki energy and that we open our minds and acknowledge even the smallest of sensations.

Ji-gam begins in our hands, which are a particularly sensitive part of our bodies. The hands are the place where Jin-ki, the essence of energy, is most readily activated. Later, once we become proficient at Ji-gam, our practice reaches a depth where we are able to place our minds completely in one place, even without trying particularly hard, as an energy center forms in the Dahn-jon.

When we practice Ji-gam for the first time, we feel external Ki in the form of sensations like fever or heat, or what seems to be a magnetic force. Later, when that sensation deepens, we can feel blood flowing in our veins. With more intense concentration, even blood flowing in the capillaries is felt. Once Ji-gam takes place in our entire

Training for Concentration

The Zen use of koans, which focus the mind on a single riddle, and the ascetic practice of intentionally causing pain are both training methods for promoting concentration.

bodies, we sense each of our cells filled with energy, living and moving. We arrive at a state of mental unity, in which our bodies and minds are one. Once we feel energy and blood circulation is invigorated in the palms of our hands (Jang-shim), bottoms of our feet (Yong-chun), and Lower Dahn-jon, we can maintain this awareness of energy even while we practice Dong-gong. Frequently practicing feeling Ki in our normal lives helps with Jung-gong as well as Dong-gong practice. For the person whose awareness of the Dahn-jon is weak, Ji-gam training can be particularly helpful in activating the heat of this energy center. The next practice involves the simple method of feeling energy in the palms of our hands and the soles of our feet, where the body's external Dahn-jon centers are located, and in the Lower Dahn-jon, which is one of the body's internal Dahn-jon centers. The Ki sensed at first is external Ki felt on the surface of the skin. With repetition, however, these sensations grow more intense and clear. Immersed in this feeling of Ki, we find that our brainwaves fall into a pattern of relaxation, our minds become very peaceful, our bodies and minds relax, and we are able to feel even more intensely the internal Ki that is beginning to stir in our bodies.

Ji-gam Training for Awakening the Sixth Sense

As bioenergy, Ki cannot be touched or seen with the naked eye. A "sixth sense" is needed to feel or see Ki, not the five senses we use in our daily lives. Ji-gam is a basic method for awakening this sixth sense.

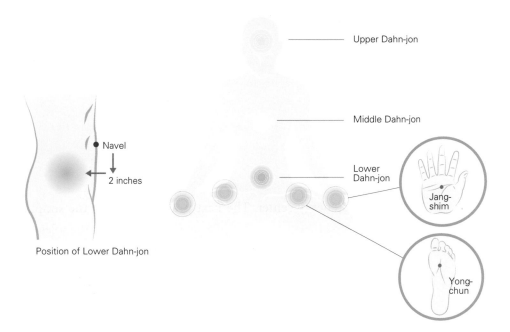

Upper Dahn-jon

Middle Dahn-jon

Navel

2 inches

Lower Dahn-jon

Jang-shim

Yong-chun

Position of Lower Dahn-jon

Internal Dahn-jon and External Dahn-jon

Our bodies have seven Dahn-jon centers. Meaning "field of energy," a Dahn-jon is a place where Ki is collected and stored. The Dahn-jon is a three-dimensional system existing at the energy level rather than the physical level of our bodies. Consequently, it does not consist of fixed individual points, nor is it seen anatomically. The practitioner, therefore, must learn to sense the precise location of these centers through training. The Internal Dahn-jon centers are the Lower Dahn-jon located in the lower abdomen, the Middle Dahn-jon located in the chest, and the Upper Dahn-jon located in the head. The Jang-shim points located in the palm of each hand and the Yong-chun points located on the bottom of each foot together comprise the four External Dahn-jon Centers. The word Dahn-jon, when used alone, usually refers to the Lower Dahn-jon.

Jang-shim

When the fingers are curled as if making a lose fist so that their tips touch the palm, the place between where the tips of the ring finger and middle finger touch the palm is the Jang-shim.

Yong-chun

When the toes are curled toward the bottom of the foot, a large V-shaped wrinkle forms there. The Yong-chun is located about at the point of the bottom of the V. The name means the point where primal Ki gushes out like water from a spring.

Feeling Energy in the Hands

The Yong-chun and Jang-shim points are major channels through which energy enters and leaves our bodies, gateways through which the energy of the universe is supplied to the human body. First, before beginning training for feeling energy, it is important to sufficiently relax mind and body.

First, rub your hands together vigorously until your palms feel hot. Then clap at least 50 times. The feeling of the Jang-shim points will become even more vivid as blood circulates vigorously through the entire palms of both hands. When clapping, spread your hands wide like fans to ensure all of both palms are thoroughly stimulated.

Comfortably relax your entire body so there is no tension in your neck, shoulders, arms or chest, and relax your mind, as well. Press your palms together in front of your chest and focus on the feelings in your palms.

Continuously thinking about the feeling of warmth in the palms leads naturally to concentration. Focus on your hands, not missing even the slightest sensation felt there.

At first, you will feel body heat, and then may get warm and cool sensations. Feel the blood that has left your heart flowing along your arteries to your hands. You will feel the pulse of blood flowing in your hands, and may get other sensations, as well.

Continue to focus your awareness on the palms of your hands as you slowly move them about 5 to 10 cm apart. In your hands you experience sensations such as warmth, tingling, and what feels like magnetic force or pressure. Your hands even feel as if they were floating in the air.

Maintaining this feeling, slowly move your hands apart as you inhale and move them together as you exhale. It is important to relax and do this slowly and naturally. Once you have no trouble concentrating, you can do this regardless of how you are breathing.

You will even feel a strong energy field, soft like jelly, forming between your hands. If this sensation becomes intense, move your hands apart even farther and focus on changes in the Ki energy occurring as the distance between your palms increases.

You will feel your hands become like magnets, pushing against and pulling on each other. This sensation is very subtle at first, but with continuing concentration it gradually grows intense and clear. Move your hands farther apart once the sense of Ki energy becomes intense. Follow the flow of Ki energy with your hands. Feel its currents and enjoy the feeling.

Feeling Energy in the Feet

A weakening lower body is one of the signs the body is growing old. As the lower body weakens with age, the flow of Ki and blood there stagnates and is blocked. To feel Ki in the Yong-chun points located at the bottoms of the feet, our legs must be sufficiently warmed up. Meaning, "primal Ki gushes like a spring," the Yong-chun is one of our body's important accupuncture points.

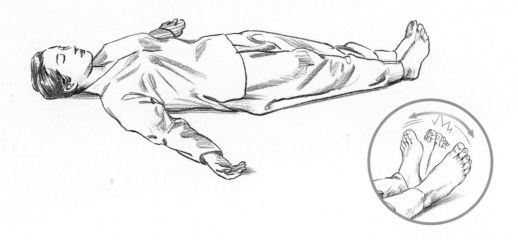

1 Lie down with your legs straight and your feet together. Tap your feet together, repeating this 100 to 500 times.

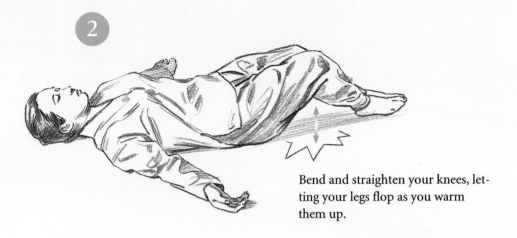

2

Bend and straighten your knees, letting your legs flop as you warm them up.

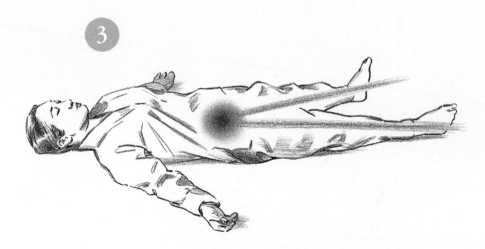

3

 Spread your legs about shoulder width apart and release all tension from them, comfortably relaxing your entire body. With your mind focused on the soles of your feet, imagine you are breathing through them. When you inhale, have the breath come in from the soles of your feet up to the Dahn-jon, and when you exhale, have the breath leave your body through your legs and out the bottoms of your feet. As you slowly repeat this breathing technique, you will get various sensations, like tingling at the bottoms of your feet, heat, a prickly feeling, or the feeling that the area around the soles of your feet is surrounded by fog.

Feeling Energy in the Dahn-jon

The Lower Dahn-jon is one of our body's three internal Dahn-jon centers (Upper Dahn-jon, Middle Dahn-jon, Lower Dahn-jon). Normally when we refer to the Dahn-jon, we mean the Lower Dahn-jon. For the Ki-sensing exercise outlined below, it is good to adopt a standing posture, and to tense the lower abdomen as little as possible.

1 Spread your feet shoulder width apart and bend your knees to approximately 15 degrees. With both palms facing the Dahn-jon, repeatedly move them slowly toward the Dahn-jon and then away from it. Breathe very comfortably and feel Ki in the Dahn-jon.

2 Once you feel the Ki to a certain extent, move your hands in a clockwise direction, maintaining the feeling of energy lining your hands to your Dahn-jon.

3 With your hands about 2 inches away, slowly move your lower abdomen and feel the Dahn-jon.

2. Energy from the Mind

Jin-ki : Pure cosmic energy

Ki energy flows in the human body in three ways. These are called "Won-ki (primal energy)," "Jung-ki (refined energy)," and "Jin-ki (Pure energy)" If Won-ki and Jung-ki are said to be energies produced even without concentrating the mind, then Jin-ki is an energy created through mental concentration. This Jin-ki is the energy used by Dahnhak Ki-gong. When we focus our minds on the Dahn-jon, energy appears in the Dahn-jon; when we focus on the hands, energy appears in the hands.

The first type of Ki energy is Won-ki. This term refers to energy passed down through the generations, which humans receive from their parents when they are born. The second type is Jung -ki which we obtain by eating and breathing. The third type, Jin-ki, is obtained through mental concentration and training, and can be considered the quintessential energy.

Jin-ki is obtained when we concentrate our awareness and breathe deeply. When we inhale, pure cosmic energy, Jin-ki, enters our bodies. The power to take in cosmic energy as Jin-ki and to circulate it within the body is the power of the focused mind. Jin-ki can be controlled by the human will because it is energy obtained through concentration. Try to feel Jin-ki using the following method.

Feeling Jin-ki

Focus your awareness on the center of your palm. Use your willpower to imagine it becoming warmer than other parts of your hand. With time, the heat at the center of your palm grows more intense. The temperature of this spot feels higher than the temperature of other parts of your body.

This heat reflects a collection of Jin-ki produced by focused awareness. Jin-ki collects where you concentrate your awareness, in whatever part of the body you focus.

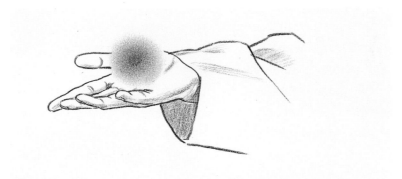

Ui-su Dahn-jon: Using the Will to Defend the Dahn-jon

A good way to train Jin-ki is to live life every day always in a state of conscious awareness. Maintaining an optimistic, tranquil attitude and concentrating on every word and deed while focusing the mind on the Dahn-jon in the lower abdomen is called "Ui-su Dahn-jon," or using the will to defend the Dahn-jon.

Another good way to train Jin-ki is to focus on the Dahn-jon with the anus contracted, the mouth closed, and the tongue resting comfortably against the roof of the mouth.

3. Basic Posture for Dahnhak Ki-gong

Sang-heo Ha-sil |
The upper body is relaxed; the lower body, solid.

Although the mind is important, posture, too, is very important for gathering energy. The movements introduced here correct our body postures before we begin Ki-gong in earnest.

The position of the hands when doing Ki-gong is not particularly restricted, but that of the legs comes as an application of the basic posture. Adequately training the basic posture allows us to do precise, solid, full movements with balance, and without a break in the flow of energy even while moving.

When performing Ki-gong, we maintain a Sang-heo Ha-sil posture, relaxing the upper body and tensing the lower body with the navel as the dividing line between the two. To create a body that is balanced in terms of Ki, we must relax comfortably to eliminate tension in the muscles at the back of the neck and to ensure there is

no tension in the upper body. In this state, we move naturally, riding the flow of energy. With a lowered center of gravity, however, the lower body carries the weight of the upper body, causing it to be filled by solid energy from the soles of the feet to the Dahn-jon.

Most modern people have stiff upper bodies and weak lower bodies due to the continuing mental tension in which they live. The movements introduced here are simple, but they strengthen the lower body, relax the upper body, and facilitate the accumulation of Ki.

Space between the Legs

The space between the legs varies. Generally, the easiest, most basic posture involves spreading the feet about shoulder width apart. This posture is not particularly hard, so it is easy even for beginners. If beginners start training with the feet spread too far apart, the energy of the Dahn-jon and lower body will be scattered, which

could actually result in a loss of energy, so they should avoid being overly ambitious.

The best posture is the one that can obtain the greatest effect in the shortest period of time, the one that can collect energy in the Dahn-jon, and also circulate it to the entire body. In other words, it is a posture that automatically results in the accumulation and circulation of Ki. The width of the feet should be such that the legs do not feel overly tensed and energy does not feel as if it is being scattered. The interval between the feet varies according to the practitioner's level of training. Shoulder width is good for beginners; those who have developed proficiency should gradually spread their legs a little wider. Our bodies remember familiar postures, so they can maintain stable, correct stances even while moving quickly.

Angle of the Feet

Forms include the Number Eleven Stance, in which a person stands with both feet parallel, the Inverted V Stance, in which a person stands with the toes pointing inward, and the V Stance, in which a person stands with the toes pointed considerably outward. Generally, the Number Eleven Stance and Inverted V Stance are used in Ki-gong training. This is because they tighten the knees and hips, gathering energy.

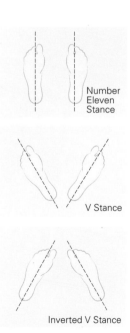

Number Eleven Stance

V Stance

Inverted V Stance

If we carefully examine the gaits of young children and the elderly, we find that, generally, they take the form of the Number Eleven Stance or a posture similar to this with the toes pointing outward about 15 degrees. When the legs lose strength and the stomach protrudes, resulting in deformed musculature, people walk in an V Stance (duck walk). This is a poor posture that causes deformation of the knee joints. The weight of the upper body causes bones to deform into the shape of the letter "O." In other words, this can lead to a warping of the bones in the shins below the knees.

Angle of the Knees

The degree to which we bend our knees varies according to the type of Ki-gong involved and to our level of training. The intensity and effects of training depend on how much we bend our knees. If we stand up with legs completely straight, the area around our knees becomes tense and our bodies fail to relax adequately. Consequently, we bend our knees naturally when we do Ki-gong. The degree to which we bend them, however, varies according to our level of training, as does the angle at which we spread our legs.

Beginning Level Stance

In this stance, the knees are bent to approximately 15 to 30 degrees. This is the easiest stance and is not difficult even if trained for several hours at a time. It is recommended for people with less physical strength, the elderly, and arthritis patients who have weak knees. Beginners start with this stance and gradually bend their knees a little more as their proficiency grows.

Intermediate Level Stance

In this stance, the knees are bent to approximately 50 degrees. The legs are bent so that the knees form a straight line with the toes, or bent a little more so that the toes are not visible. A normally healthy person can train in this stance after finishing with the beginning level stance.

Advanced Level Stance

This stance is very difficult, with the knees bent deeply to approximately 90 degrees. The lower body is bent deeply and so is somewhat tense, but the upper body is completely free of tension. Unless a person is sufficiently skilled, he or she will find it difficult to last more than two or three minutes in this stance, and may actually become tired because the body is overly tense. People with less physical strength and the elderly should not attempt to go too far with this.

Six Basic Postures

All of the six basic postures introduced below are for cultivating fundamental Ki-gong skills before beginning the actual practice of Ki-gong. Most Ki-gong movements are slightly modified from the following six postures. As a consequence, properly practicing the basic postures contributes significantly to Ki-gong.

Il-si Posture: One Beginning

With precise practice and training of this posture, the hips are automatically aligned and the body stands straight. Breathing also naturally descends to the Dahn-jon, so the energy of the lower body is readily gathered there.

1 Let your arms hang naturally or hold your palms together in front of your chest. Relax your shoulders. Leave space under your armpits, enough room for about one egg. As you relax your arms, contract your ribs on both sides slightly, allowing Ki to sink readily to your Dahn-jon.

2 Relax your mouth and lightly touch the tip of your tongue to the roof of your mouth at the back of your top teeth. This will connect as one circuit the Governor Vessel passing through your back with the Conception Vessel flowing at the front of your body.

3 Put your feet straight together, bend your knees to about 15 degrees, and keep your big toes and heels on the ground, with your weight centered on the Yong-chun.

4 Relax your upper body and, with the muscles of your buttocks and legs, gently pull the perineum forward and upward. Align the Baek-hoe, Hoe-eum, and Yong-chun.

Il-bon Posture: One Origin

Adopting this posture, you can train for as long as you want. It is effective for training internal Ki. It is also good for strengthening the lower body and eliminating arthritis.

1 From the Il-si posture, move your left foot so that your feet are about a shoulder width apart and bend your knees to about 15 degrees. Hold your palms together in front of your chest or otherwise position your hands as appropriate. Keep your back straight with your chest relaxed and slightly concave, ensuring there is no tension in your upper body at all.

2 Prevent your buttocks from protruding by slightly tucking your tailbone forward and upward toward the Hoe-eum.

3 Ensure that your feet are completely parallel, pointing neither outward nor inward. Also bring the Baek-hoe, Hoe-eum and Yong-chun into complete alignment.

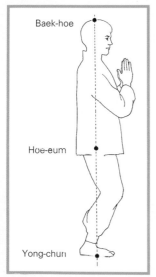

Hoe-eum: Between the genitals and anus
Baek-hoe: Crown of the head

Practitioners with visceroptosis should hold this posture with their toes pointed inward about 15 degrees.

Patients with high blood pressure or neurasthenia should train with their toes pointed outward approximately 15 degrees. This has the effect of causing energy to sink to the Dahn-jon.

Il-chun Posture: One Heaven

This posture is also called a "horse stance." In this stance, which is somewhat difficult, the upper body and surface of the ground should be perpendicular to each other. It is not suitable for the elderly or people with less strength to hold for a long period of time because it requires physical strength and stamina.

1 From the Il-bon Posture, move your feet farther apart (to approximately one and a half to two shoulder widths). Lower your stance very slowly, keeping your spine perpendicular to the ground, as if you have a weight on a string hanging from your tailbone and want to keep the weight from moving.

2 Bend your knees so that a right angle is formed at the knee between your thighs and shins. In this posture, ensure that there is absolutely no tension in your upper body, shoulders, Dahn-jon, or lower back.

Il-shim Posture: One Mind

In this posture, particular care should be taken to ensure that the upper body does not lean to the front or back. The back should be kept straight so that a vertical line is formed connecting the Baek-hoe and the Hoe-eum.

1 From the Il-bon Posture, move your right (or left) foot to the back, maintaining a distance of about one shoulder width between your back and front feet.

2 Bend your back leg to approximately 90 degrees, with the ball of your back foot resting on the ground and the heel raised.

3 Block upward with one hand while pressing outward with the palm of your other hand at the height of your Middle Dahn-jon. Bend your elbow slightly at this time.

Il-in Posture: One Humanity

In this posture, although one knee is bent, the upper body should be held erect, leaning neither to the front nor to the back, so that a line connecting from the Baek-hoe to the Hoe-eum is perpendicular to the ground.

1 From the Il-chun Posture, bend your right (or left) knee and straighten your other leg.

2 Block upward with your right (or left) hand and push outward with your other hand, at the middle or lower levels. Your line of sight points toward the extended hand.

Il-ji Posture: One Earth

This is also called a "front stance." The upper body is kept erect with the center of gravity at the Dahn-jon.

1 From the Il-chun Posture, turn your upper body to the right (or left).

2 Bend your front knee and straighten your back leg, keeping the bottom of your back foot in contact with the surface of the ground.

4. Training Ki in the Body

Internal Ki

To train the muscles, bones, and Ki simultaneously, we must feel and train the internal Ki flowing in our bodies, rather than exercises that train only the muscles. Internal Ki is present in the bones, organs, and meridians of the body, and in every one of its cells. Won-ki and Jung-ki do exist in the body as internal Ki, but once these are expended, our energy fails as we age if we do not train. Moreover, the minds and bodies of modern people are being ruined by mental labor, overwork and stress that expend Ki, and by a lifestyle far removed from nature.

Excessive emotional changes due to greed and passion also exhaust Jung-ki and spoil Won-ki. Training internal Ki keeps disease-causing energies from invading our bodies. Even if they do enter, they are soon driven out by internal Ki. Our health is maintained and illnesses heal naturally as a result.

Feeling Internal Ki

To feel and train internal Ki, we have to see to it that Jung-ki is changed into Jin-ki as we engage in correct Ki-gong movements (body control), breathing (breath control), and concentration (mind control). The movements introduced below are internal Ki training methods that are simple and yet very effective, allowing even Ki-gong beginners to feel and train internal Ki easily. If we use the energy in our bodies along with breathing, our respiratory volume is increased and our bodies overflow with energy.

Stand with your legs in the Il-bon Posture and extend your fingers with both arms hanging comfortably at your sides. In this state, concentrate on the tips of your fingers. If you continue to focus your mind on the tips of your fingers, you will feel them become hot. You can feel your pulse and a growing heat.

Spread your fingers like a fan and continue to focus your mind. You feel a pressure about to burst from the tips of each of your fingers and your hands seem to grow larger. Feel the energy traveling into your hands as it pours out of your fingertips. Practice this constantly until the feeling in your fingers is vivid and intense.

Now that you have felt the energy in your fingers, stand with your legs and knees turned inward so that your toes face each other. Extend your arms so that your fingers point toward the ground.

At this time, turn your hands so that your palms face inward, with your thumbs facing the front, and spread your hands like fans. Extend your fingers forcefully like spears and focus on the sensation of Ki you feel in them.

In this posture, take a breath and then hold it, continuing to focus on the ends of your fingers. Along with the sense of pressure about to burst from your fingertips, feel the heat spreading to your entire body.

Exhaling to a count of three, straighten your legs and send Ki forcefully to your fingertips. Breathe in and then perform this action again as you breathe out. Repeat this about 10 times. You can also concentrate the Ki energy with a strong yell when you exhale to a count of three.

This time, slowly raise both hands above your head as you inhale and bend your knees at the same time.

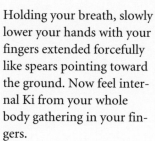

Holding your breath, slowly lower your hands with your fingers extended forcefully like spears pointing toward the ground. Now feel internal Ki from your whole body gathering in your fingers.

Exhaling, straighten your legs, and at the same time extend your fingers forcefully, as if they are spears you are thrusting into the ground. As you do this, gather as much Ki as possible and send it out through your fingers. At this time, you can also count to three and then further focus Ki energy with a yell.

Internal Ki Training through Tension and Relaxation

Internal Ki training is a basic, yet important practice for becoming energized in Dahnhak Ki-gong. With constant daily practice, regardless of our level of training, at some point we suddenly feel an unshakable physical and mental stability, surprising even to ourselves, and cultivate hardy physical and mental strength.

1 Adopt the Il-chun Posture, with both hands held at the Dahn-jon.

2 As you breathe in, raise your hands to your chest, with your palms facing the sky.

3 Exhale and lower your hands to your Dahn-jon, with your palms facing the ground. Repeat this three times.

Most important in internal Ki training is posture. The legs should form an "11" if possible, and care should be taken to keep the buttocks from protruding when the knees are bent. If the lower back is curved, causing the buttocks to stick out, tension leaves the lower body, making effective practice difficult. When repeating these movements, the practitioner should also keep in mind that he or she is to maintain a Sang-heo Ha-sil posture, the lower body solid and the upper body relaxed, consistently from beginning to end.

4

Spread your arms to the side, raising them so that they are horizontal at chest height. Point the palms of your hands downward, straighten your fingers, and relax your shoulders at this time.

5

Regardless of your breathing, slowly move your arms together toward the front, bend your elbows slightly, and bend your knees at the same time, so that your legs form a 90 degree angle.

6

Straightening your legs, returned to your original position. Continuing to repeat these movements fills your muscles and bones with internal Ki.

5. Points to Keep in Mind When Practicing Dahnhak Ki-gong

Relaxation

Relaxation of body and mind is more important than anything else. The excessive burden or ambition to do well from the very beginning must be avoided. Being filled with ambition and letting this cause us to overtrain or expect quick results actually causes tension in the body's muscles and has an adverse effect on training. We should begin with an attitude of resting comfortably, relaxing and loving our bodies. We enter training in earnest, then, once our practice accelerates to a certain degree.

Open Mind

We should approach training with an open mind, discarding our own ideas and preconceptions. We can better feel and control energy when we approach training with the unclouded mind of a little child. We have trouble concentrating and experience many busy thoughts during training because we are attached to our own, narrow ideas. At least in the moments we are practicing, we should lay down such attachments and empty our minds.

Devotion

Comfort should be accompanied by seriousness. Seriousness means devotion. If we devote ourselves entirely to each and every movement, this is intention and mind control.

Constancy

Once we begin training, we should practice steadily every day, even if just for five minutes at a time, rather than trying to practice for a long time all at once.

Naturalness

Do not be obsessed with form. Remember that genuine practice involves finding a natural comfort of body and mind. When we feel comfortable, we can see, feel, and enjoy the Ki and blood moving in our bodies. In this process, we come to love our bodies and to feel truly alive.

Slowly and Softly

Dahnhak Ki-gong, unlike other Ki-gong systems, has an unusually large number of circular, calm, soft movements. The trick is to slowly focus the mind on the movements we are doing. If we rush and move quickly, rather than being filled with energy, our bodies tire as a lack of oxygen causes the production of lactic acid.

Precautions

· If severe vibration occurs when you perform Ki-gong, exercise self restraint. You can stop the vibrations consciously. If the vibra-

Vibration

In some cases, the body trembles intensely when acupuncture points once blocked with stagnant energy open up for the first time. This phenomenon occurs when, as we perform Ki-gong, new energy pushes its way into our bodies, opening blocked meridians. We can compare this to the violent shaking of a hose caused by water pressure when it is connected to a faucet and the water is turned on suddenly. However, too much vibration causes energy to be wasted, so we should refrain from vibrating for too time. This can be controlled consciously.

tions occur while training with your eyes closed, open your eyes and take deep breaths, slowly moving your awareness to your Dahn-jon. Vibrations, if intense, can cause energy to be exhausted.

· Do not train when you have overeaten or are hungry.

· Avoid wearing tight clothing or tightening your belt too much.

· Avoid training too much all at once or using too much tension. Being too ambitious and training for long hours in the beginning stages, when Ki is not yet circulating adequately in the meridians, can cause side effects if the body is unable to handle the energy.

· Do not overly concern yourself with any miraculous or spiritual experiences you may have during training. Neither fear nor its opposite, obsession with these experiences, are good for training. Just look at it as another phenomenon of training and move on to the next level of your practice.

Do-in Exercises

Doing Do-in (meridian) Exercises for about 10 to 20 minutes before beginning full Ki-gong training is effective for relaxing both body and mind. Do-in Exercises gently stretch and relax tense muscles and stiff joints, facilitating distribution and circulation of Ki within the body. These exercises also help us feel Ki and move with the flow of energy. Advanced practitioners as well as beginners should do Do-in Exercises regularly.

Emptying the Mind

One who has emptied the mind so that nothing material weighs on it,

naturally has an unclouded mind. From this mind, a keen light like that

of gold and jade shines forth. In this emptiness of mind, truth and

energy are created, allowing you to, on a large scale, understand how

the universe moves, and on a small scale, understand how a small parti-

cle of dust comes into being. These truths and energy are completely

empty yet divine.

- From *Cham-jun-gye-gyung*

Chapter 3

Dahn-gong

丹功

Nothing is impossible with great dedication;
no problem insurmountable with a constant heart.
Dedicated practice and training open the gates
of Heaven and the way to Earth.

1. Brilliant Stillness in Movement

I. Brilliant Stillness in Movement

With deepening Ji-gam training, Ki flows strongly in the body, manifesting as powerful, martial-art-like movements. We call this "Dahn-gong." In freestyle Dahngong, movements manifest themselves differently from person to person, without a set framework.

Even in freestyle Dahn-gong, however, certain specific forms appear, depending on the flow of Ki. These forms were organized based on the principles of Kigong training into the five stages of Dahn-gong. Training begins with the Basic Form (Gi-bon-hyung), and then progresses gradually, according to the practitioner's level of training, to Ki Accumulation (Chuk-ki-hyung), Belt Vessel (Dae-maek-hyung), Conception and Governor Vessel (Im-dok-maek-hyung), and Microcosmic Circulation (So-ju-chun-hyung) forms.

The movements of the Dahn-gong Basic Form, in which arms and legs are extended forcefully, correct skeletal and muscular misalignment and develop basic physical strength for other Ki-gong training to take place later on. Once the framework of basic postures is established by the Basic Form, we develop good energy through the Ki Accumulation Form. When we have accumulated sufficient Ki, we move on to the advanced stage of Ki circulation training. Once energy circulation is developed through the Belt Vessel and Conception and Governor Vessel forms, we progress to the next form, Microcosmic Circulation. In this book, we introduce the Basic Form and Ki Accumulation Form, which beginning and intermediate practitioners can use for training.

As a martial art that is strong yet gentle, we can feel a compressed power in Dahn-gong's softness. Included even in strong actions are movements in which we momentarily relax. Tremendous power is emitted in those instants as Ki is radiated.

One of the appealing aspects of Dahn-gong is that even long periods of training do not exhaust us. Energy is accumulated continuously in the Dahn-jon during training because we move with the flow of energy rather than use strength recklessly.

Except for cases such as Tai Chi or Taekgyeon, which conceal tremendous power in relaxed movements, most martial arts are a series of very fast, violent fighting techniques. Dahn-gong's goal is not defeating or destroying an opponent, but rather adapting to the flow of energy to control and use it, and thereby understand the mind, which is the essence of energy. In other words, it is mental training for learning how to control ourselves, not a tool for controlling or attacking an opponent.

With Dahn-gong, we can approach our true objective only if we practice with a knowledge and understanding of Ki. Without a knowledge of Ki, it would simply be mimicking movements. If we practice Dahn-gong with breathing, movement, and awareness united, we can feel our Jang-shim, Yong-chun, and Dahn-jon centers flushed with heat, our bodies soaked with sweat.

Controlling tension during Dahn-gong is important. Although it is incorrect to flex our muscles too much, Ki is not generated if we are too relaxed and do the movements too softly. If we feel strength draining out of our bodies after doing Dahn-gong, then we have trained incorrectly. It is acceptable to perform movements thinking of them as about 30 percent strength and about 70 percent Ki accumulation. It is a good idea to thoroughly learn the basic postures introduced in the second chapter of this book before beginning regular Dahn-gong.

2. Dahn-gong Gi-bon-hyung: Basic Form

The Dahn-gong Basic Form is made up of the most frequently used and fundamental movements in Dahn-gong, hand forms, steps, and energy-circulation methods in Dahn-gong.

Repeating the Basic Form can lead to deeper concentration during training and allow us to feel Ki readily. Once trained precisely, Basic Form becomes a foundation for infinite creating in freestyle Dahn-gong. Musculoskeletal alignment is corrected and our bodies are strengthened as we train the Basic Form, maintaining precise postures, until it is thoroughly ingrained in our bodies.

In the case of beginners just starting Dahn-gong, the energy of the Dahn-jon rises, flowing backwards, and makes the face flushed and the breathing shallow if their bodies are too tense and their breathing is erratic during training. Accordingly, they should begin by abandoning any ambition to perform the movements perfectly and practice moving with the energy, bodies relaxed and comfortable. Then they will finally experience stillness in motion in each and every movement of Dahn-gong.

1. Make Fists

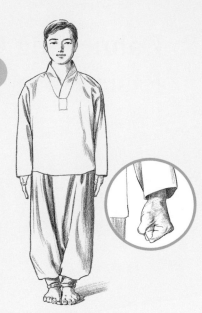

Stand in an Il-si Posture. Relax your upper body and tense your lower body so that it feels as if you are pushing upward and support-ing your body with the entire soles of your feet. Inhale and make a loose fist with both hands, and then relax your fists, straightening your hands, as you exhale. Gather energy as you repeat this three times.

2. Beginning Posture

Extending your left foot forward in a semicircle, spread your feet shoulder width apart. You are changing the distance between your feet while maintaining a posture with your knees bent.

Points to Remember

Make sure that your body does not lean forward or backward, putting excessive pressure on your knees or lower back. With all postures in Dahn-gong training, the lower abdomen should be slightly tensed, the center of gravity maintained at the Lower Dahn-jon, and power rooted through the soles of the feet.

Il-si Posture   Il-bon Posture

Stepping in the Dahn-gong Basic Form generally employs movements trained in the Il-si and Il-bon postures.

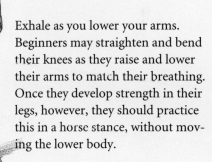

4

Exhale as you lower your arms. Beginners may straighten and bend their knees as they raise and lower their arms to match their breathing. Once they develop strength in their legs, however, they should practice this in a horse stance, without moving the lower body.

3

Inhale as you raise both arms to shoulder height.

Points to Remember

Beginning Posture is for initiating circulation of internal Ki in our bodies. Through this movement, we create respiration and energy conditions appropriate for doing Dahn-gong. The Beginning Posture movement promotes the flow of energy along the body's vertical meridians.

The breathing method in Dahn-gong, except for the Beginning and final Breathing postures, involves exhaling with 30 percent of the breath left in the lungs. In the Beginning Posture, however, breathing is controlled so that 80 percent of the last breath is exhaled, with 20 percent retained by the lower abdomen.

3. Press Forward

Inhaling, turn your hands palms up and raise them to your armpits.

Points to Remember

As you lift your hands, also raise along the Governor Vessel energy stored in the Dahn-jon. All movements using the palm (where the palm presses forward), including Press Forward, should be done with slight tension, as if moving a great mountain.

Exhaling, press both palms forward. Contract your lower abdomen at this time.

Points to Remember

When pressing the hands forward, ensure that energy from the Dae-chu point travels out through both arms to reach the Jang-shim points. Lightly press forward with the energy loaded in the Jang-shim points, as if pushing a great mountain.

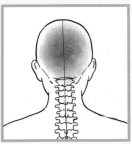

Dae-chu Point: Located between the seventh cervical vertebra and first thoracic vertebra. The bone that protrudes the most when you bend your neck forward is the seventh cervical vertebra, and the bone immediately below it is the first thoracic vertebra.

4. Open the Chest

Inhale as you cross your arms in front of your chest.

Exhale as you extend your arms out to the side, palms facing outward.

Points to Remember

When you open your chest with your palms, do so with great force and spirit, as if dividing the sea.

5. Turn and Press Left and Right

1

As you inhale, lift your left foot and adopt a cat stance (feet close together, heel of one foot lifted with toes touching ground), slowly turning your upper body to the left.

2

Press forward with the center of your right palm while moving your left hand as if pressing down on the energy of the Dahn-jon or the ground. At the same time, circle your left foot slightly to the rear as you move your feet apart.

3

Exhale as you press forward fully with the center of your right palm. Bend your front leg and straighten your back leg. Stand straight with your upper body erect.

Of the six basic movements, this one trains stepping for the Il-ji Posture, which is also called a front stance.

Il-ji Posture

Now repeat the movement in the opposite direction.

6. Single Hand Press to the Front

Continuing from the previous movement, press forward with the center of your palm as you turn your body to the front. Look in the direction your hand is moving.

Switching hands, repeat the previous movement.

7. Knife Hand Block

Turn your right palm upward as you cross your arms and do a twisting block to the right. At the same time, move your left hand as if pressing down on the energy of the Dahn jon or the ground.

Again, crossing your arms, this time turn your left palm upward and do a twisting block to the left. Move your right hand in front of the Dahn-jon, as if pressing down on the energy of the ground.

8. Il-in Posture

1 Lower your stance as you extend your left leg and bend your right knee. At the same time, cross your arms in front of your chest.

2 Extend your left arm downward along your left leg, bending your hand back at the wrist, palm out. Move your right hand as if blocking upward. Look to the left.

3 Shift your weight to your left leg and, at the same time, cross your arms in front of your chest.

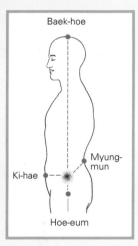

Baek-hoe and Hoe-eum Points

4 Bend your left knee and straighten your right leg as in the previous movement. At this time, the right hand extends downward and the left hand blocks upward.

Points to Remember

The line from the Baek-hoe to the Hoe-eum should be kept perpendicular to the ground to prevent the upper body from leaning to the front or back.

9. Open the Chest

Repeat the previous Open
the Chest movement.

10. Open the Ah-mun

1 Inhale as you raise your hands behind your head and cross them at the Ah-mun point.

2 Exhale as you slowly press your hands outward to the sides.

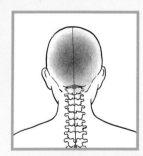

Ah-mun Point: Located between the first and second cervical vertebrae. It is situated on the center line of the neck and head, in the depression where the neck and head meet.

11. Bend Forward at the Waist, Twist the Arms

Bend forward at the waist, look-ing downward, as you inhale. Twist both arms backward so that your palms face upward as you exhale.

12. Hold up the Sky

Continuing from the previous movement, raise your upper body into an erect position. Bend your knees to lower your buttocks and waist, and use both of your hands to pull up energy from below, as if embracing a large ball.

Slowly straightening your legs, press both hands upward simultaneously as if holding up the sky, and focus your Ki by yelling, "Yap!" upward.

13. Gather Energy

1 Continuing from the previous movement, cross your wrists over your head and then lower them to your Dahn-jon along a central line.

2 Inhaling again, spread your arms outward to the sides and raise your hands above your head.

3 Gather energy from your Baek-hoe to your Dahn-jon, exhaling as you lower your hands.

14. Bring the Feet Together and Clap

3 Clap your hands as you bring them together above your head.

2 Drawing a huge circle toward the outside with your hands, raise them above your head.

1 Bring your feet together and lower your hands, crossing them in front of your Dahn-jon.

15. Closing Breath

1 Keeping your hands together, lower them in front of your chest as you inhale.

2 Turn your hands palms down and move them downward to your lower abdomen (Lower Dahn-jon) as if lightly pressing on the ground. Exhale about 80 percent of the air in your lungs at this time.

3 Drop your head and arms as you relax your hands and the back of your neck, exhaling all of the air (20 percent) left in your lungs. Connecting this with movement number 14, repeat this series up through Closing Breath two more times.

3. Dahn-gong Chuk-ki-hyung: Ki Accumulation Form

When we train the Dahn-gong Ki Accumulation Form, our bodies overflow with life and vitality as they are filled to the bursting point with energy, like rubber balloons. In this state, our bodies move quickly and agilely with appropriate tension, and our concentration and awareness are deepened.

The Dahn-gong Ki Accumulation Form is training for the purpose of accumulating Ki. Although movement of the upper body in the form is softer than in other training, a solid lower body must be maintained. This is referred to as Sang-heo Ha-sil. We must always keep this point in mind when performing the Dahn-gong Ki Accumulation Form.

In the Ki Accumulation Form, the space between the legs and the degree to which they are bent varies according to the practitioner's level of training. With greater proficiency, practitioners increase the space between their legs and the angle of their knees, working to develop flexibility, strength, and stability.

Progress in Kigong training depends on how constantly we practice. We will be able to achieve our desired goals if we practice ceaselessly, applying precise principles and methods.

Stimulating Energy

Before we begin the regular Ki Accumulation Form, we perform basic Ki-circulation movements for stimulating the energy in our entire bodies, including our hands and arms, chest, neck, and legs. Make Fists and Beginning Posture movements are performed as they are in the Dahn-gong Basic Form.

1. Make Fists

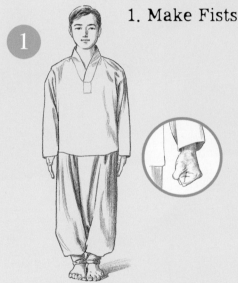

2. Beginning Posture

Standing in an Il-si Posture, make a fist with both hands as you inhale and then relax your fists, straightening your hands, as you exhale. Stimulate Ki beginning in your hands as you repeat this three times. Open the Baek-hoe and Yong-chun points to link in your body the energies of Heaven and Earth. Calm your mind and keep the center of energy in your Dahn-jon.

Extending your left foot forward in a semicircle, spread your feet shoulder width apart and stand looking at the distant heavens.

Inhale as you raise both arms to shoulder height, and then exhale as you lower them. Repeat this movement three times. Do not exhale completely on the last repetition; breathe out only 80 percent of the air in your lungs.

3. Single Hand (Right Hand, Left Hand) Presses toward Heaven

Exhale, and as you do so, lower your raised hand. As you inhale again, press upward toward the sky with your left hand and downward toward the ground with your right hand. As before, use only about 80 percent of your strength.

Inhale and press upward toward the sky with your right hand and downward toward the ground with your left hand while lightly flexing the Dahn-jon. Do not completely extend your arms at this time, but give your elbows a slight, natural bend, using only about 80 percent of your strength. Stop your left hand at the height of the Lower Dahn-jon.

4. Two Hands Press toward Heaven

Inhale and lift both of your hands, pressing them toward the sky. Use only about 80 percent of your strength at this time. Take care not to allow your buttocks to protrude, and lightly spread your palms to stimulate energy in your hands.

Points to Remember

Ensure that energy does not rise upward as you lift your hands. The key is to raise your arms without using excessive strength, and to keep the mind centered on the Dahn-jon.

5. Open the Chest

Continuing from the previous movement, exhale as you lower your hands toward your chest, and then inhale once again as you cross your hands in front of your chest.

Exhale as you extend your arms to the sides. Using only about 70 percent of your strength, ensure that energy subtly permeates your body.

6. Open the Ah-mun

Inhale as you raise both arms, and then exhale as you open the Ah-mun point at the back of your neck.

Continuing this movement, perform Open the Chest, pressing to the sides as you circulate Ki through your shoulders and arms.

7. Turn the Hips

Supporting your body with your left leg in a stable stance, raise your right arm and right leg and rotate them in a large semicircle to the outside as you return them to their original positions. Inhale as you lift your arm and leg and exhale as you lower them.

3 This time, raise your opposite hand and foot and perform the same large, circular motion on the other side.

4

Repeat this movement three times: right side, left side, and then right side, in that order.

Points to Remember

This movement helps circulate Ki through the lower body by loosening the hips, where energy is easily blocked during full-body Ki circulation. Relax tension in the hips and arms as you stimulate energy in the legs.

8. Crane Stance

1 From the previous hip rotation movement, continue the technique without placing your foot down completely.

2

3 Bring your foot back under your knee without lowering it to the ground and stand on one leg, maintaining your balance.

4 Lower your foot to the ground and stand with your feet shoulder width apart. With your arms at shoulder height, move as if lightly grasping the energy of the ground and your body, completing the Beginning Posture movement.

Goose Posture

This posture brings to mind a vision of flying geese. Like geese flying off in search of their homes, the movement suggests an intention to recover the true nature of humanity. It is also called the "Bok-bon Posture," which has the meaning of returning to the source. Viewed from a martial arts perspective, this movement comprises simultaneous attack and defense.

1

From the closing movement of the Beginning Posture, turn your head to the right and, at the same time, bring your hands up to your armpits.

2

Bring your right foot back beside your left foot and stand with your right heel lifted off the ground. Place your weight on your left foot at this time.

3

Make a semicircle as you step forward with your right foot and place your weight evenly on both legs. Raise your arms as you inhale.

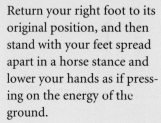

Return your right foot to its original position, and then stand with your feet spread apart in a horse stance and lower your hands as if pressing on the energy of the ground.

Turn your head to the front and, at the same time, bring your hands up to your armpits.

5

4

Lower your arms as you exhale. The key here is to move slowly and feel a taut energy, like a rubber band being stretched up and down. Raise and lower your arms six times.

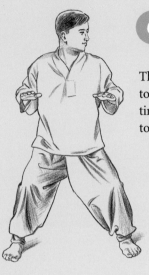

6

This time, turn your head to the left and, at the same time, bring your hands up to your armpits.

7

Bring your left foot back beside your right foot and stand with your left heel lifted off the ground. Place your weight on your right foot at this time.

8

Make a semicircle as you step forward with your left foot and then raise and lower your arms six times.

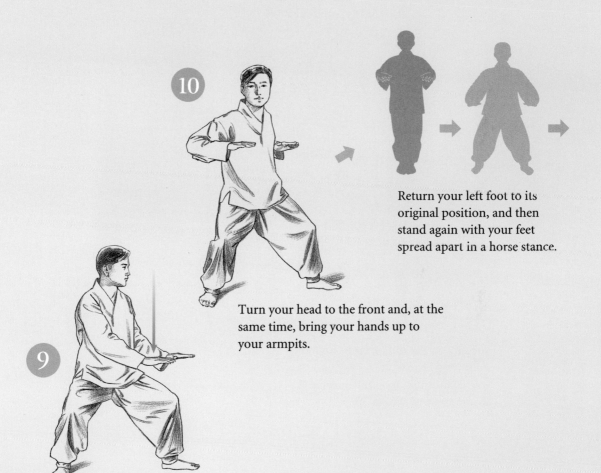

Return your left foot to its original position, and then stand again with your feet spread apart in a horse stance.

Turn your head to the front and, at the same time, bring your hands up to your armpits.

Mermaid Posture

This movement brings to mind a vision of a mermaid returning to the Halls of the Dragon King. The Halls of the Dragon King symbolize a world in which the true nature of humanity is realized. Here, the image of humanity dedicated to recovering its true nature is given form in the picture of a swimming mermaid.

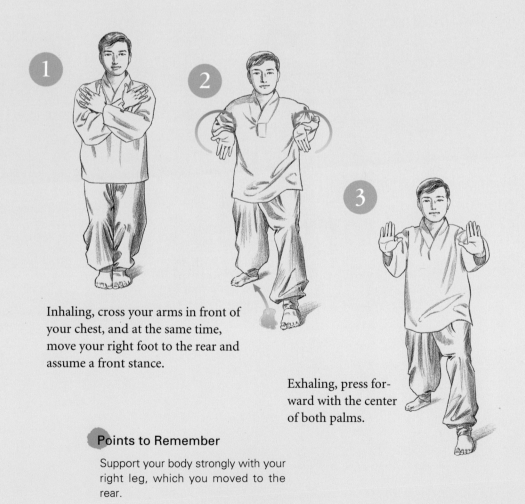

Inhaling, cross your arms in front of your chest, and at the same time, move your right foot to the rear and assume a front stance.

Exhaling, press forward with the center of both palms.

Points to Remember

Support your body strongly with your right leg, which you moved to the rear.

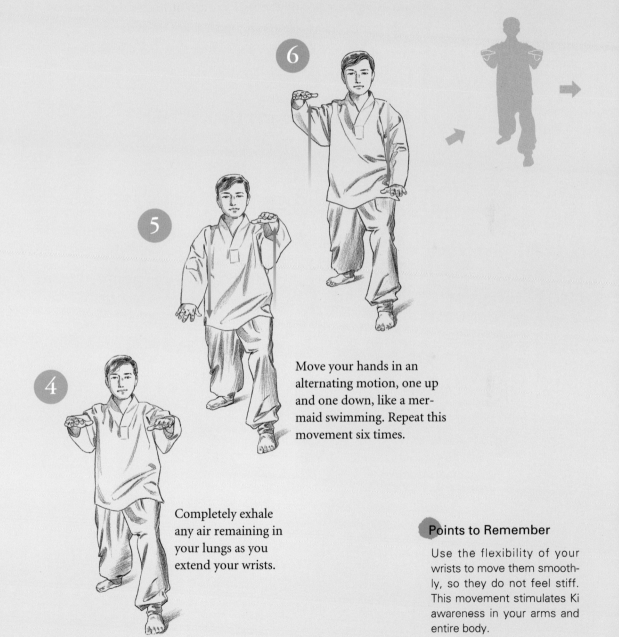

Move your hands in an alternating motion, one up and one down, like a mermaid swimming. Repeat this movement six times.

Completely exhale any air remaining in your lungs as you extend your wrists.

Points to Remember

Use the flexibility of your wrists to move them smoothly, so they do not feel stiff. This movement stimulates Ki awareness in your arms and entire body.

Gathering Posture

This posture pushes out and blocks internal obstacles dormant within us, including various emotions, feelings of injury, ambitions, etc. These movements are basic to martial arts and also contain philosophy. If internal Ki is strengthened centered on this philosophy, awareness grows at the same time.

1. Middle, Lower, and Upper Dahn-jon Press

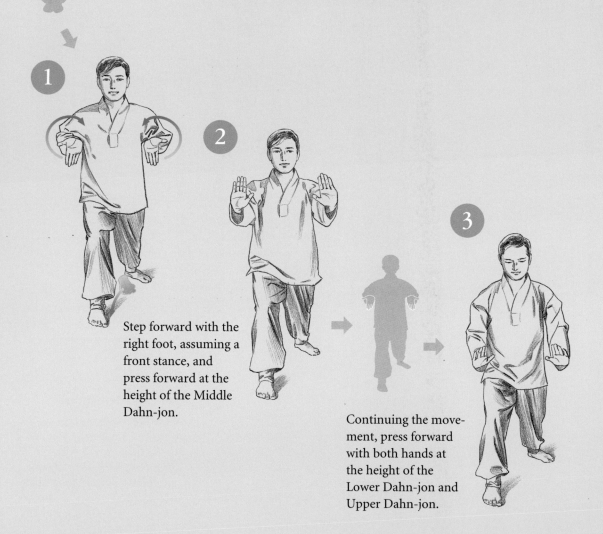

Step forward with the right foot, assuming a front stance, and press forward at the height of the Middle Dahn-jon.

Continuing the movement, press forward with both hands at the height of the Lower Dahn-jon and Upper Dahn-jon.

Again, do a Middle Dahn-jon press.

Cross your arms at your Middle Dahn-jon, open your chest and press forward. Repeat this two mor times.

2. Knife Hand Block

Place all your weight over your left foot, and with your right foot lightly touch the ground using only the tip of your big toe. In this position, do three knife hand blocks from the outside in, with the right hand, the left hand, and then the right hand.

3. Fist Block

Move your right foot into a horse stance, make a fist with both hands, and perform a fist block from the inside out three times, with the right hand, the left hand, and then the right hand.

Block three
times from the
outside in.

Now in the opposite
direction, lower and
block to the inside with
your right fist, which
you just used to block to
the outside.

Self-Realization Posture

This movement contains the intention to find and realize the true nature within ourselves. It is performed very slowly and purposefully. Finding our true nature is important, but so is realizing the self and sharing it with the world. The Self-Realization Posture gives form to this truth.

1 Continuing from the final fist block, stand in a horse stance with both your hands held as fists at your hips. Inhaling, open your right hand and slowly bring it to cover your left fist.

2 Exhaling, open your left fist and press forward with the center of the palm of your hand. At the same time, form your right hand into a fist and bring it to your right hip.

3 This time, as you inhale, bring your left hand to cover your right fist.

When ending this set of movements, hold your breath and press forward with the center of your left palm, then count to yourself, "One, two, three," and focus your Ki with a yell, "Yap!"

Exhaling, open your right fist and press forward with the center of the palm of your hand. At the same time, form your left hand into a fist and bring it to your left hip. Repeat this two more times.

Breathing Posture

With this closing posture, we return to the breathing we use in everyday life by exhaling the last 20 percent of the air in our lungs, which remained in our bodies during Dahn-gong.

Breathe in as you bring your hands together over your head.

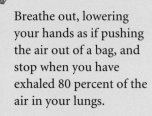

Breathe out, lowering your hands as if pushing the air out of a bag, and stop when you have exhaled 80 percent of the air in your lungs.

Simultaneously relax your hands and shoulders, drop your head, and exhale the remaining 20 percent of the air in your lungs. With your head dropped toward your chest, feel the sensation being transmitted to your spine. Repeat these movements three times.

Sincerity

Merely continuing without rest is not the same as continuing with intense dedication. It is as the gap between wavering human desire and determination to gather a full measure of the power of the Tao: Though small at first, it soon widens into the gulf between Heaven and Earth.

- From *Cham-jun-gye-gyung*

Chapter 4

Ilchi Ki-gong

一 指 氣 功

When the dragon is taken into the Dahnjon,
Heaven, Earth, and humanity become one.
When profound methods and principles are
shared with the world, Heaven and Earth are
renewed, and human becomes ascending dragon.
Once staying in the clouds, the dragon returns
to Earth to make the world a better place.

1. Philosophy and Principles of Ilchi Ki-gong

Philosophy of Ilchi Ki-gong

Ilchi Ki-gong is an ideal combination of physical and mental training. Permeating its eight sets are the philosophy and spirit of the Korean people as well as kinetic principles necessary for training the body.

The eight sets of Ilchi Ki-gong express the philosophy and principles of creation, education, and civilization. The principles of creation, education, and civilization gave birth to a philosophy and spirit of enlightenment and became the founding ideology of a nation in Korean antiquity. The principle of creation involves the concept that there are three intrinsic elements of harmony, rather than a dichotomous structure of competition and confrontation. It is a universal principle of life and enlightenment, in which humanity, nature, and the cosmos blend together. The principle of education involves sharing with the world and educating people in this philosophy and principle of enlightenment. According to the principle of civilization, this philosophy of enlightenment forms the basis of a social system in which all members live to perfect their lives as human beings. Each and every movement of Ilchi Ki-gong contains such profound philosophical principles.

A trap into which Ki-gong practitioners readily fall is remaining at the level of Ki once they learn to feel and harness it, as if Ki were everything. This is only the beginning of genuine practice, however. As our practice deepens, we come to experience a great number of miraculous, spiritual phenomena. When this happens we encounter great confusion, like a person looking for a needle in a haystack, unless we are armed with the right mindset and correct principles.

So practitioners need the right mindset and correct principles, and a proper teacher, all of which serve as guides. Proper philosophy, principles, and teachers act as guides which the practitioner can use during training to conquer confusion and reach his or her goal. This is why the spirit and philosophy contained in Ki-gong training are so important.

Characteristics of Ilchi Ki-gong

Lifting heavy weights to train the muscles is not the only way to train the body. By performing movements that slightly angle the joints and by practicing breathing techniques as we gather and release Ki, even in a short period of time, our bodies are warmed up, energy circulates, and we can train internal Ki. Beginners can readily develop Ki awareness merely by repeating these simple movements. Although performing the same actions, the advanced practitioner with a deep level of training is able to enter a blissful state of deep concentration through these simple movements. This is the essence and true beauty of Ilchi Ki-gong.

Another characteristic of Ilchi Ki-gong is that infinite changes are possible within a single movement. The basic movements of this method are simple, but infinite creation and change are possible once Ki is felt within them. With music and soft energy, the sets become a dance; with breathing and gathering of Ki, they become Ki-gong; and with application of potent Ki energy, they become martial arts training in self defense.

Unlike ordinary Ki-gong or martial arts techniques, the lines of movement of Ilchi Ki-gong are harmonious, smooth, and very soft. Ki-gong for self defense or fighting involves many blocking and striking types of movements. Employing aggressive movements and energies without a proper philosophy is likely to lead the temperament of the practitioner in that direction as well. With Ilchi Ki-gong, if we train each movement intent on the spirit contained within it, harmonious, peaceful energies are produced, and in no time at all, our bodies and minds are suffused by the principle of harmony.

2. Eight Sets of Ilchi Ki-gong

Training Principles of Ilchi Ki-gong

Ilchi Ki-gong is the essence of Dahnhak Ki-gong, designed so that modern people can learn it readily and yet obtain the greatest exercise benefit possible. The eight sets of Ilchi Ki-gong have a high level of perfection in terms of kinetics. Made up of movements that involve turning, pushing, pulling, raising, and lowering each part of the body, they produce a well-balanced physique.

Major movements comprise rotational motions and simple actions that involve angling the joints and squeezing out energy. Slowly performing simple movements as we gather and release Ki through respiration causes the entire body to be flushed with heat, sweat, and circulating energy.

The following table shows the relationship between body control (kinetic aspects), breath control, and mind control achieved by practicing the eight sets of Ilchi Ki-gong.

Set	Body Control (Kinetics)	Breath Control	Mind Control
Chwi-ryong Sam-sik	Vertical movements raising, lowering arms	Inhale when raising, exhale when lowering arms.	Gather energy to Dahn-jon.
Chun-in Sam-sik	Sang-heo Ha-sil with upper body relaxed, lower body solid	Inhale going out, exhale coming in.	Circulate energy to Heaven, Earth, and humanity.
Jo-hwa Sam-sik	Movements raising, lowering, pushing, pulling arms	Inhale when moving in semicircles, exhale when pushing at end-point.	Feel harmony of body and mind.
Gyo-hwa Sam-sik	Regulates balance of spine, muscles, nerves; shoulders, wrists do rotational movements.	Inhale when arms go back, exhale when arms go out.	Develop energy as if teaching energy paths to body.
Chi-hwa Sam-sik	Balanced lateral movement, circulation of energy in six major joints	Inhale when arms go back, exhale when arms go out. Inhale when pulling back, exhale when closing in front of chest.	Perform movements naturally along energy pathways. Feel energy expanding to infinity. Feel Heaven, Earth, and humanity becoming one (oneness with the universe).
Gae byuk Sam-sik	Open and close arms.	Inhale when opening arms, exhale when closing arms.	Open and close energy (mind). Turbid energy replaced by clear energy with energy circulation during respiration.
Hwa-ryong Seung-chun	Adjustment of thoracic vertebrae and ribs.	Breath-holding techniques	Raise energy along Governor Vessel to fill Geuk-cheon points. (Achieve state of Su-seung Hwa-gang, with water energy ascending, fire energy descending.)
Hae-jeo Chim-su	Movement for relaxation	Inhale when raising arms, exhale when lowering arms.	Return all energy to Dahn-jon.

Ilchi Ki-gong Training Method

There are several ways to train Ilchi Ki-gong. The first method is to perform the movements very slowly while feeling the energy after learning the form. Another method is to speed up, performing the movements rapidly.

Once we are comfortable with all the movements, we can practice the form from beginning to end without stopping, or we can concentrate on just one set, repeating it and getting a thorough feel for it.

One good method, as a type of Dahn-jon training, is to work the body by holding one posture for an extended period. The most common approach is to unite breathing, movement, and awareness, feeling stillness in motion and moving naturally like flowing water.

Just going through the motions as we practice Ilchi Ki-gong is virtually meaningless. It is important that we understand and appreciate the purpose of each movement.

Chwi-ryong Sam-sik: Seize the Dragon (Repeat 3 Times)

Set One

"Chwi-ryong Sam-sik" refers to a stance for seizing the dragon. Here, "dragon" symbolizes the Ki writhing in our bodies. Once Ki is accumulated in the Dahn-jon through training, energy moves within us like a writhing dragon. As you perform these movements, think about pressing this Ki into the Dahn-jon.

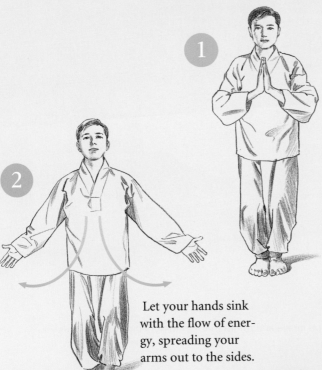

1 Hold your palms together in front of your chest, standing with your legs as you would in the Il-si Posture. Put your feet together so there is no space between your knees and ensure that your buttocks does not protrude backwards to much. Stand with your upper body relaxed and erect, without leaning forward or backward.

2 Let your hands sink with the flow of energy, spreading your arms out to the sides.

3 Continue to inhale as you raise your hands above your head, gathering energy. Hold your breath when your palms touch above your head. Look at your hands at this time.

4 Still holding your breath, lower your arms and start moving your hands apart -- wrists first, fingertips last -- beginning in front of your chest. Spread your palms and press downward, as if pushing energy into the Dahn-jon. Keeping your knees together, bend your legs as you press downward with your hands. Repeat this process three times.

Turn your hands inward, bending them back at the wrist slightly, as you press them down in front of your Dahn-jon, so that the outer edges of your wrists press outward. Also lift the ends of your little fingers, turning them inward slightly. Feel the energy generated in your hands. The elbows should be bent to about 45 degrees. Turn your wrists inward as far as they will go. Hold your upper body erect, being careful not to lean backward. Keep your shoulders relaxed and tense only your fingers.

Points to Remember

Turn your hands inward as you inhale and return them to their original positions as you exhale. Straightening the knees at this time is also key. Feel the energy leaving your wrists as you return them to their original positions.

With your wrists bent and holding your breath as much as possible, feel strong tension forming in your fingers. When you feel a strong pressure and heat ready to burst from your fingertips, exhale and straighten your wrists and knees, relaxing your posture. This is a very simple movement, but if they repeat it many times, even beginners can readily acquire Ki awareness.

When you raise your little fingers, imagine them lifting a huge weight. You can also feel your toes tensing at this time.

Chun-in Sam-sik: Heaven and Humanity (Repeat 3 Times)

Set Two

Heaven and Humanity is a set for sharing the energy gathered in the Dahn-jon with Heaven, Earth, and humanity by Seize the Dragon. The hands are moved in a circle three times. The first time signifies love for Heaven; the second, love for the Earth; and the third, love for humanity. This set is imbued with the spirit of Heaven, Earth, and humanity, so perform these movements with a comfortable, compassionate smile on your face and with a heart full of love.

1 From the final position of Seize the Dragon, move your right foot so that your feet are shoulder width apart.

2 Turn your upper body and eyes to the right, place your left hand in front of your Dahn-jon and move your right hand in a clockwise circle. You may move both hands together at this time.

3 Move your hand in a circle three times, and as you do so, think to yourself, "Heaven... Earth... Humanity..." Inhale as your hand moves to the outside and exhale as it moves to the inside.

4

Continuing from the previous movement, bring your right foot next to your left foot.

5

6

Next, move your left foot so that your feet are shoulder width apart and turn your upper body to the right. Stop your right hand in front of your Dahn-jon and move your left hand in a counterclockwise circle three times with an attitude of love for Heaven, Earth and humanity. Feel the energy in your palms and Dahn-jon. (You may also move your right hand.)

Points to Remember

You should maintain your posture and balance when moving left and right. Keeping the lower body solid and the upper body relaxed is the most basic principle of this posture.

When you move your hands in a circle, your upper body should move, also, naturally following your hands. You should be careful, however, because awareness and energy will not be focused if you attempt to do this consciously.

Jo-Hwa Sam-sik:
Creation (Repeat 3 Times)

Set Three

The Creation set contains the meaning of harmony between people and harmony between people and nature. In this set, our bodies are filled with energy, we share love with the world, and we feel our bodies and minds achieving harmony. Creation trains the lower body, making it strong. Keep your upper body erect and your lower body solid, and ensure that your line of sight is directed toward your fingers. The Ki in our bodies is vitalized through this movement.

1

Continuing from the final movement of Heaven and Humanity, turn your eyes to the right and bring your left foot behind your right foot, adopting an Il-shim Posture. Raise the heel of your left foot about 45 degrees and hold your trunk erect. At the same time, move both hands smoothly downward in a semicircle, and then raise them to face the right side. Lightly bend your right wrist and turn your left palm upward, holding it in front of your chest.

The distance between your left and right feet should be about one and a half times the length of one of your feet, and your feet should be angled 90 degrees to each other. Bend your knees as appropriate for your level of conditioning.

Points to Remember

Be careful not to allow your buttocks to protrude or your upper body to lean forward. Maintain the height of your stance as you move your body like flowing water, left and right. Feel the Ki as you circle your arms, moving very smoothly as if in water. This is very effective for developing Ki awareness in your hands.

Keeping your feet in the same position, lower your arms in a semicircle in the opposite direction, and then return to position (1) to complete one series of movements. Repeat this series three times.

Now return your left foot to its original position, so that you are in a horse stance, and then move your right foot behind your left foot in the opposite direction. Move your arms as you did previously, back and forth three times.

Gyo-hwa Sam-sik: Education (Repeat 3 Times)

Set Four

The Education set involves accepting the energy of Heaven, circulating and sending it out into the world, and then once again accepting energy from Heaven and gathering it within ourselves. These movements teach our bodies energy pathways. Through them, we learn to use the energy of Heaven, Earth, and humanity to greatly expand the energy of our bodies. This set has the effect of correcting the function of the organs and aligning the joints and spine.

1 Continuing from Creation set, bring your right foot back to its original position so that your feet are shoulder width apart, and at the same time turn your right palm upward and stretch it out back and above your right shoulder. Simultaneously bring your left hand in front of your chest (Middle Dahn-jon), with the palm turned upward. Follow your extended hand with your eyes and also turn your upper body naturally in the direction your hand travels.

2 Twisting your right arm, rotate your right wrist once counterclockwise and bend it so that your right palm faces upward.

6

Bring your right arm back the same way, describing a circle with your hand as it comes under your armpit, and then raise it to make another circle above your head.

5

Stretch out your arm fully to the front, lightly touching your ribs with your hand as it moves forward.

4

3

From this position, pull your right hand back toward your ribs under your right armpit.

Bring your hands in front of your chest. The palms always face upward at this time, as if holding a dish.

Continuing on the opposite side, move your left hand the same way you did your right hand. Perform these movements three times, alternating between your left and right sides.

Points to Remember

Ensure there is no break in the continuity of the movement when you thrust your hand, with wrist bent, toward the front from the ribs underneath your armpit. The key is to do the movement smoothly, with the muscles of your shoulders relaxed.

Unlike the right side, people frequently have a difficult time performing the movement correctly on the left side. This reflects a difference in our nervous systems and sense of balance between the left and right sides, so be sure to train your weaker side thoroughly.

Chi-hwa Sam-sik:
Civilization (Repeat 3 Times)

Set Five

In this set, we perform the movements of Education set simultaneously with both arms. A characteristic of the Civilization set is that it expands Ki to infinity, spreads energy to the ends of the Earth, and develops awareness significantly. When performing these movements, we focus on becoming one with the universe, on the principle that Heaven, Earth, and humanity are one. We train with our awareness focused on the Dahn-jon, our hearts full peace and love.

1

Adopt a horse stance with your knees bent appropriately for your level of conditioning. Bend your arms slightly, with your palms facing upward at chest level.

2

Inhale as you spread your arms out to the left and right from in front of your chest.

5

Stretch your arms forward, with you wrists bent inward. Breathe out naturally at this time.

4

Bring your hands from behind your back forward to your armpits.

3

Bend your upper body forward and twist your arms, moving them to the back so that both palm face upward.

Move your hands to your armpits, making circles with your palms facing upward.

Make large circles once above your head as you lower your hands to the front of your chest, continuing to move as if drawing figure eights.

Points to Remember

Civilization Triple Set opens the three major joints of the upper body and three major joints of the lower body, facilitating Ki accumulation. As we repeat the movements slowly, feeling each of our joints, our skeletons and muscles are adjusted and Ki and blood circulation are improved.

When you spread your hands out to the left and right, think of energy rising from the Yong-chun points at the soles of your feet, passing through your legs, waist, and shoulders, and moving out into your fingers. In the opposite direction, when retracting your hands, think of energy gathering from your fingers to your Dahn-jon. These movements become self-defense techniques if filled with powerful Ki and become a dance if performed softly.

Gae-byuk Sam-sik: Open a New World (Repeat 3 Times)

Set Six

In Open a New World set, after passing through the process of creation (Jo-hwa), education (Gyo-hwa), and civilization (Chi-hwa), we find a new world opening before us. Like the renewal of Heaven and Earth, the Ki in our bodies is renewed when turbid energy is replaced by clear energy as the movements of the set open and close. This training involves concentrating the awareness in the Dahn-jon, and feeling and connecting Ki in the Yong-chun points as well as the hands.

1

From the final position of Civilization set, pull in the right leg, bringing the feet together, and put your palms together in front of your chest.

As you inhale, lower your hands in front of your Dahn-jon with the backs of your hands facing the front. Hold your breath and focus your mind on the Dahn-jon to gather energy there. Ensure that your buttocks does not protrude, and keep your knees and legs completely together.

2

3

As you exhale, spread your arms to the sides with your palms facing upward, sending turbid energy out of your body. Repeat this movement with the arms opening and closing three times.

Points to Remember

Relax your forehead and contract your chest slightly. Tension will leave your body if you drop your shoulders naturally and adjust your posture appropriately.

Pull in clear energy, accumulating Ki, when you gather your hands in front of your Dahn-jon, and send turbid energy out through your hands when you spread them to the sides.

Hwa-ryong Seung-chun: Dragon Rises to Heaven

In the Dragon Rises to Heaven set, we show that the world has been renewed and that humanity has become the dragon ascending to Heaven. This set involves gathering Ki in the hands, raising it up along the Governor Vessel and spine, and collecting it in the Geuk-chun points. This is the dragon ascending to Heaven and staying in the clouds.

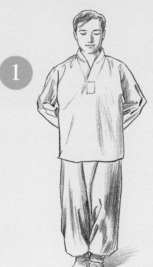

1 Place the backs of your hands against your lower back, standing with your hips pulled forward, knees slightly bent, chest lifted, and shoulders pulled back.

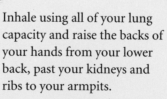

2 Inhale using all of your lung capacity and raise the backs of your hands from your lower back, past your kidneys and ribs to your armpits.

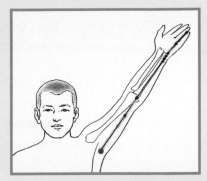

Geuk-chun Point: Located in the armpits, on the Heart Meridian.

4

Exhale, and as you do so, extend your wrists, lowering your hands slowly to your ribs. This whole process is one repetition. Repeat this set about three times, depending on your condition.

3

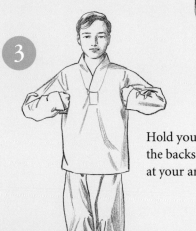

Hold your breath with the backs of your hands at your armpits.

Points to Remember

Bring your hands to your armpits, pulling your elbows toward your ribs, and lift your chest, opening it as much as possible. This posture correctly aligns the skeleton and nervous system, which transmit energy from the brain to the internal organs along the spine and ribs, and facilitates the flow of Ki deep within the bones.

Generally, the upper chest is tensed to strengthen heart and lung function.

Hae-jeo Chim-su: Return to the Water

Set Eight Return to the Water symbolizes the ascended dragon living in the clouds. Finish by gathering energy to your Dahn-jon, matching this with the movement of your hands, as you imagine the peace and serenity of a place deep in the ocean.

1 From the last position of Dragon Rises, turn your palms over to face the ground.

2 As you inhale, raise your hands along your ribs to your chest.

3 As you exhale, lower your hands along the same path. Close by lowering your energy to the Dahn-jon and Yong-chun points.

Points to Remember

Focus on your breathing as you raise your hands and on the movement of your hands and flow of Ki within your body as you lower them. Unite mind and Ki so that your energy sinks along with your hands.

When you finish training, always end by lowering your energy to your Dahn-jon.

A Teaching on Heaven

That blue expanse is not Heaven; Heaven is not that distant, empty sky. Heaven has neither form nor foundation, neither beginning nor end. It has neither up nor down, neither circumference nor direction. It appears empty, and yet is full. There is nowhere it is absent, nothing it does not embrace.

- From *Sam-il-shin-go*

Flow of Ki and Major Meridians

經絡

Humanity is in the midst of Ki; Ki is in humanity.
In all of creation, nothing is not Ki.

Meridians: Pathways of Energy Flowing in the Body

Meridians and Ki Circulation

Meridians are channels along which energy flows in our bodies. As the land has waterways -- large and small rivers and streams -- bringing life to all things, so, too, the human body has large and small pathways along which energy flows. Meridians, however, are not anatomically visible to the eye. Nor are the meridians through which energy flows identical with the blood vessels through which blood flows. Flowing water is living and unspoiled. The energy flowing in our bodies has a nature similar to that of water. When our bodies overflow with energy, the flow of Ki and blood is enhanced, and we feel light and full of vitality. Conversely, if our energy is weak, or is blocked and flows poorly, blood circulation is also adversely affected; blood congestion occurs as dead blood congeals. This is the beginning of all kinds of diseases. Physical and psychological tension blocks Ki and blood flow. When blood flow is blocked, so are the meridians, which makes Ki circulation difficult.

The practice of moving Ki gathered in the Dahn-jon through the meridians to the entire body is called "Un-ki," that is, "circulating Ki." If Ki circulation is to work well, our bodies must first be relaxed and Ki must be accumulated in the Dahn-jon. We can use intention to circulate energy through the meridians once our stiff bodies have relaxed to a certain degree, we have accumulated Ki in the Dahn-jon, and we have developed powers of concentration. Cold Ki or bad energy leaves our bodies and fundamental healing of disease takes place at this stage. We also feel new energy rising in our bodies, as well as mental stability and peace.

Ki Structure of Our Bodies

Twelve Ordinary Meridians and Eight Extraordinary Meridians flow in our bodies. The Twelve Ordinary Meridians flow at the body's surface; the Eight Extraordinary Meridians, at places a little deeper in the body. Ki normally flows through the Twelve Ordinary Meridians, but then moves to flow in the Eight Extraordinary Meridians when training causes the others to be filled to overflowing with energy. Once Ki starts flowing through the Eight Extraordinary Meridians, various powers unimaginable to normal people may manifest themselves. The Eight Extraordinary Meridians are the Conception Vessel, Governor Vessel, Flush Vessel, Belt Vessel, Yang Link Vessel, Yin Link Vessel, Yang Heel Vessel, and Yin Heel Vessel.

The Governor Vessel flows upward along the backbone to the head and controls all Yang meridians. The Conception Vessel flows downward along a central line at the front of the body, connecting the lips, throat, chest and abdomen, and controls all Yin meridians. The Conception and Governor Vessels are considered very important as the remaining 12 meridians are thought to open naturally to the flow of energy once these two meridians are opened.

Of the Twelve Ordinary Meridians, those that are Yang in character flow downward along the back, and along the backs of the arms and legs. These meridians are close to the surface of the body and are connected with hollow organs such as those of the digestive system. These organs are the stomach, large intestines, small intestines, bladder, and gallbladder. Meridians that are Yin in character are located at the front of the body and on the inside of the arms and legs. They flow upward, inside the skin. Such meridians connect with the lungs, spleen, heart, kidneys, and liver, which are solid organs of the body.

In this book we provide introductory information on the Conception and Governor Vessels, which are the most important of the Twelve Ordinary and Eight Extraordinary meridians.

Twelve Ordinary Meridians

The Twelve Ordinary Meridians are the Lung Meridian, Spleen Meridian, Heart Meridian, Kidney Meridian, Pericardium Meridian, Liver Meridian, Large Intestine Meridian, Stomach Meridian, Small Intestine Meridian, Bladder Meridian, Triple Energizer Meridian, and Gallbladder Meridian.

The names of the Twelve Ordinary Meridians vary according to

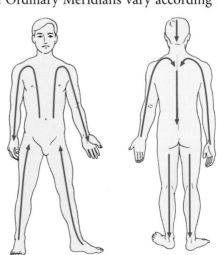

Meridians that are Yang in character flow downward along the backs of the arms and legs.

Meridians that are Yin in character flow upward along the front of the body, under the skin.

the name of the organ with which they are connected, whether they flow in the arms or legs, the time they are active, and whether they are located in a Yin or Yang part of the body.

For example, the Bladder Meridian (in Korean, literally, "Foot, Strong Yang, Bladder Meridian") flows in the foot, is located in a Yang part of the body, and is connected with the bladder. The Lung Meridian (in Korean, literally, "Hand, Strong Yin, Lung Meridian") flows in the hand, is located in a Yin part of the body, and is connected with the lungs. However, these are usually abbreviated simply, "Bladder Meridian," and, "Lung Meridian," using only the name of the associated organ. They are also referred to as Yin and Yang anterior, posterior, and lateral meridians, according to their location at the front, back, or sides of the body.

Accordingly, the Twelve Ordinary Meridians can be classified by whether they are located in the Yin or Yang section of the body: with six Yin meridians stretching out in the Yin part of the body (from the trunk to the fingers and toes) and six Yang meridians stretching out in the Yang part of the body (from the head and face to the fingers and toes). They can also be classified based on their connections to the arms and legs: with six hand meridians stretching along the arms to the fingers and six foot meridians stretching along the legs to the toes. Of the six meridians flowing in the hands, three are Yin and three are Yang. The six meridians flowing in the feet are also divided into three Yin and three Yang channels.

Most Active Times of Each Meridian

Ki flows sequentially through the 12 meridians. The organs of the body form Yin-Yang pairs. For example, the Liver Meridian (Yin) is paired with the Large Intestine Meridian (Yang). Each meridian is most active during a continuous two-hour period, and is least active 12 hours later. By observing when bodily symptoms occur, we can identify the meridian where imbalance has developed. It helps to refer to this cycle when practicing Ki-gong.

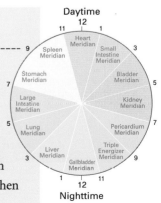

Pathways of Major Meridians Flowing at Front, Back, Sides of Body

Yin Meridians: Beginning in feet, flow to chest and outside of fingers.

Yang Meridians: Beginning in hands, flow over head, along back, outside of arms and legs.(The Stomach Meridian is an exception.)

The meridians flow in a bilaterally symmetrical way in our bodies.

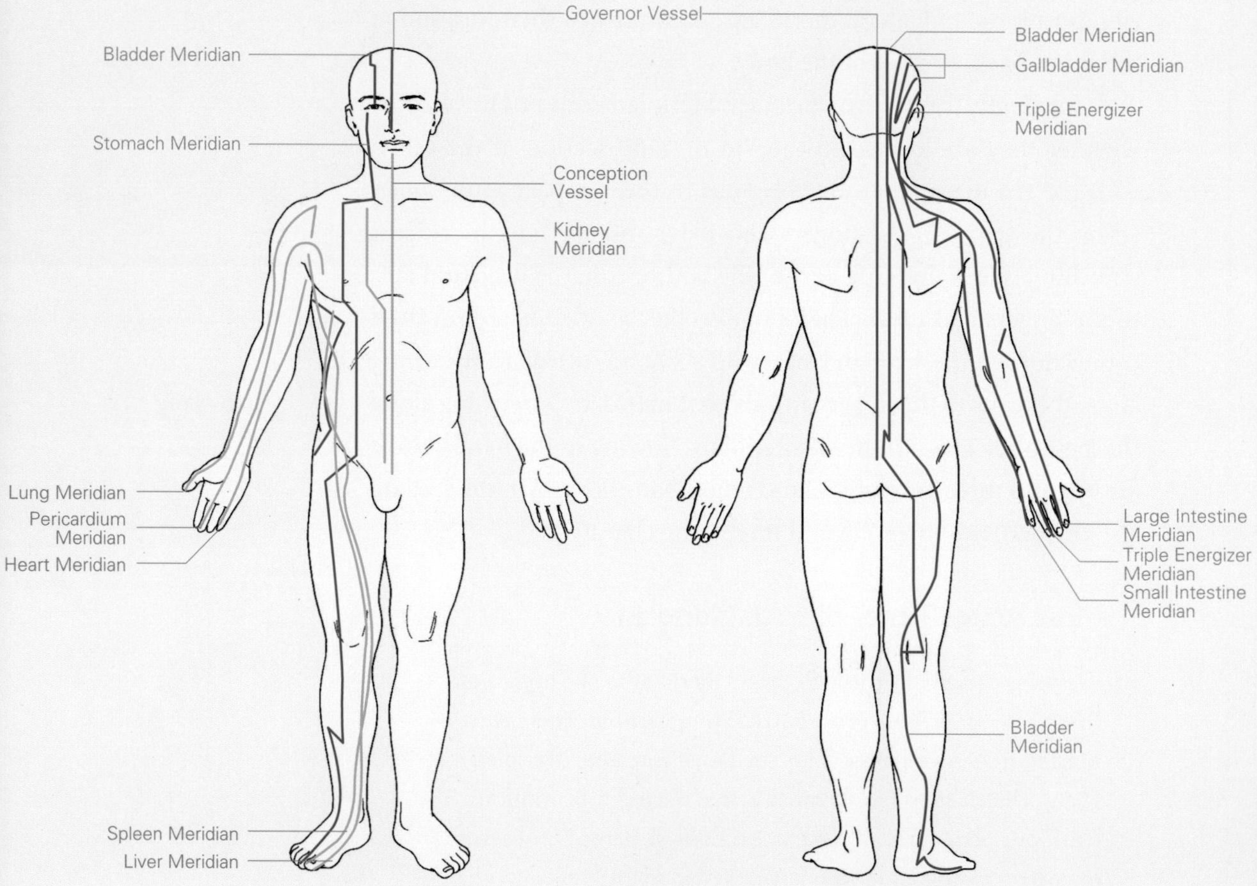

Governor Vessel
Bladder Meridian
Stomach Meridian
Conception Vessel
Kidney Meridian
Lung Meridian
Pericardium Meridian
Heart Meridian
Spleen Meridian
Liver Meridian
Bladder Meridian
Gallbladder Meridian
Triple Energizer Meridian
Large Intestine Meridian
Triple Energizer Meridian
Small Intestine Meridian
Bladder Meridian

Twelve Ordinary Meridians

- Arms
  - Three Yin Hand Meridians
    - Lung Meridian — Heart Meridian — Pericardium Meridian — Yin
    - Large Intestine Meridian — Small Intestine Meridian — Triple Energizer Meridian
  - Three Yang Hand Meridians
- Legs
  - Three Yin Foot Meridians
    - Spleen Meridian — Kidney Meridian — Kidney Meridian
    - Stomach Meridian — Bladder Meridian — Gallbladder Meridian — Yang
  - Three Yang Foot Meridians

Twelve Ordinary Meridians

▼ Anterior Meridians   ▼ Posterior Meridians   ▼ Lateral Meridians

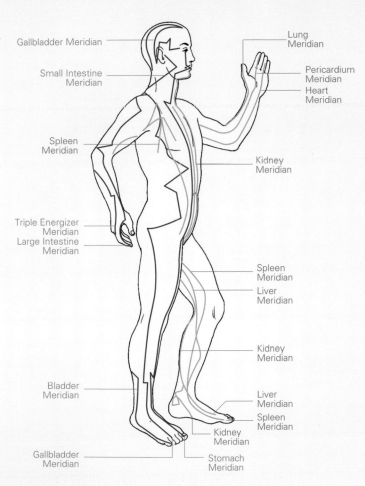

Gallbladder Meridian

Small Intestine Meridian

Spleen Meridian

Triple Energizer Meridian
Large Intestine Meridian

Bladder Meridian

Gallbladder Meridian

Lung Meridian

Pericardium Meridian
Heart Meridian

Kidney Meridian

Spleen Meridian
Liver Meridian

Kidney Meridian

Liver Meridian
Spleen Meridian

Kidney Meridian

Stomach Meridian

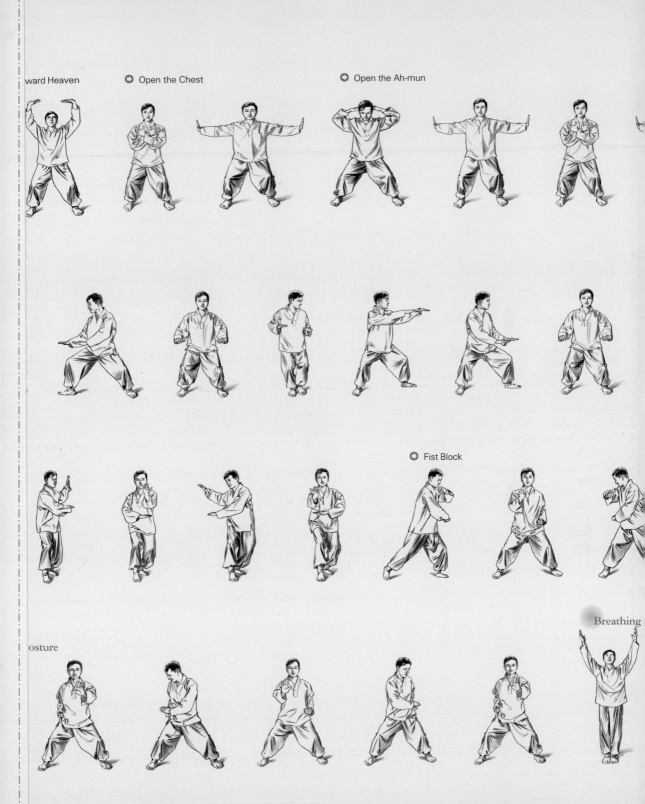

ward Heaven   ○ Open the Chest   ○ Open the Ah-mun

○ Fist Block

osture

Breathing

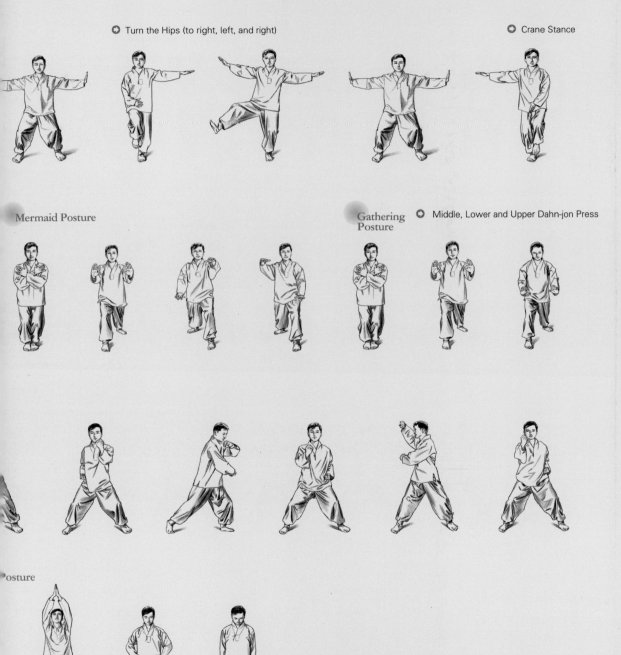

Turn the Hips (to right, left, and right)   Crane Stance

Mermaid Posture

Gathering Posture   Middle, Lower and Upper Dahn-jon Press

Posture